PROFIT
FROM YOUR
PODCAST

PROFIT
FROM YOUR
PODCAST

Proven Strategies to Turn
Listeners into a Livelihood

DAVE JACKSON

ALLWORTH PRESS
NEW YORK

Allworth Press books may be purchased in bulk at special discounts for sales
promotion, corporate gifts, fund-raising, or educational purposes. Special
editions can also be created to specifications. For details, contact the Special Sales
Department, Allworth Press, 307 West 36th Street, 11th Floor, New York, NY
10018 or info@skyhorsepublishing.com.

24 23 22 21 20   5 4 3 2 1

Published by Allworth Press, an imprint of Skyhorse Publishing, Inc. 307 West
36th Street, 11th Floor, New York, NY 10018. Allworth Press® is a registered
trademark of Skyhorse Publishing, Inc.®, a Delaware corporation.

www.allworth.com

Cover design by Mary Ann Smith

Library of Congress Cataloging-in-Publication Data is available on file.

Print ISBN: 978-1-62153-772-4
eBook ISBN: 978-1-62153-773-1

Printed in the United States of America

To Adam Curry and Dave Winer, who invented podcasting, thank you for the global megaphone that enables anyone to reach the world. To my audience (and God), who never lets me down. You are more than download numbers, more than "fans"; you are friends. You tell me when I need to improve and praise me when I get things right. In life, the one thing I value more than anything is honesty. It is not always easy to find. One of my mantras is "Constant Improvement" (it's the teacher in me), and I love that we push each other to be better people and to change this world one download at a time.

Contents

Preface
Did You Have a Lemonade Stand?

I grew up poor (I know the taste of government cheese). When I was a seven-year-old freckle-faced kid, I remember my first lemonade stand. While other kids collected G.I. Joe dolls, I collected toy banks. In junior high (before there were vending machines in schools) I would go to the local corner store and buy a pack of gum and then sell it by the piece to my friends. It was somewhat humiliating (one step above begging). I always felt like the odd man out. But I saw supply and demand, and you do what you must do. I was the only person willing to sell gum in school, and the profit margins were huge.

I would help my friend with his paper route before getting my own. All through my life, when the doors were closed, I found a way to open them. When my parents struggled financially, I found a way to chip in. I never gave up. I might want to, but I never did.

I found that the bar for excellent service was set low, and when you delivered *value* (you will hear that word a lot) and created *relationships* (get comfortable with that word as well), your audience/customers could support you. How else does a sixteen-year-old kid support a car (buying his gas, insurance, etc.) with a paper route? With my paper route I made triple what the kid before me did in tips because I would take the extra four steps to make sure your paper was dry when it was raining out. Why? Because it's hard to read a paper when the ink is all smeared, and my customers appreciated it.

You must be willing to do the other *little* things that others aren't willing to do. I didn't know it then, but I was an entrepreneur. It wasn't easy. When I got my first "real" job bagging groceries, I got fired for not talking to customers. Being the "poor" kid, I didn't have a ton of confidence (and by that, I mean none), and I was the poster child for introverts. The sixteen-year-old me would laugh if I told him I would grow up making a living talking to groups of people—but it's true. You do those little things step by step, and you get to where you want to go.

Are you like me? You're willing to do the extra work, slightly obsessing over the goal in front of you (I saved *months* for my first real guitar). You're willing to sacrifice and give up watching reruns of *Seinfeld* or *Friends* on TV. You realize life is a classroom, and you like to learn something new every day, and then apply it the next day.

If that's you, and you have a podcast, then you've found the right book. Starting a podcast is not hard. Starting a *good* podcast takes planning, focus, dedication, and time (lots of time). Zig Ziglar said, "You don't have to be great to start, but you do have to start to be great."

One last thing, as I write this, it's February 2020. Things may change by the time you read this. Please keep that in mind.

Introduction
Meet Your Author

My name is Dave Jackson, and I have been teaching technology as a corporate trainer for over twenty years. I have a bachelor's degree in education, specializing in technical education. My *School of Podcasting* show has over 2.3 million downloads. I launched my first podcast on April 4, 2005, and soon after that, I opened the doors of the School of Podcasting (schoolofpodcasting.com). I have helped tons of people launch their podcasts, have been asked to speak at conferences, and have been cited as an expert in other books on podcasting.

In 2017 I won the Best Technical Podcast in the People's Choice Awards. In 2018 I was inducted in the Academy of Podcasters Hall of Fame.

I'm writing this book as if you are sitting across the kitchen table from me. It's your typical oval table with one of those vinyl covers with a pattern. The napkin holder is in the middle of the table. Let's stay casual, shall we? I'm going to need you to focus, so quit playing with the saltshaker.

WHY I WROTE THIS BOOK

When I talk with people after they've been podcasting for a few months, I'll ask, "Are you making any money yet?" (if that is one of their goals). I often get the response, "We haven't been approached by any sponsors yet." Every time I explain the different ways to make money with a podcast, people will always say, "I didn't know you could do that," or "I didn't know that was available." This book is to let you know what is possible and what is available.

LET'S BE REALISTIC

The book is titled *Profit from Your Podcast*. It is not titled *How to Get Rich Quick Podcasting*. If it were, I'd have to triple the price and start talking about how you can escape the cubicle life and live the life of your dreams starting NOW!

If you implement the ideas in this book, I feel that you will make more money with your podcast than you are now. While there are podcasters who are making six-figure incomes, these are currently the exception and not the rule. Like many things in life, you get out of it what you put into it. A podcast about Apple products has a much better chance of making money than a podcast about Frisbee golf. All podcasts have the capability of making more money. Some have more potential than others. If you are looking to get rich quick, you may have purchased the wrong book. Scott Aukerman of *Comedy Bang! Bang!* (in the movie *Ear Buds*) states how it took two years before anyone was interested in sponsoring his podcast. Jeff Sanders of the *Five AM Miracle* podcast took three years to get his first sponsor. I often hear the phrase "three years" as an answer about monetization. I believe this is due to the fact that in year one you are figuring it out and finding your voice. In year two, you have a better understanding of your audience and deliver *value*. By year three, you've got an engaged audience who is ready to act.

I'm sure I would sell more books if the opening page read, "You can earn six figures from your basement in just ten weeks," but that's not true. It's also not true for musicians, actors, comedians, or athletes.

The Power of Podcasting

If you learn nothing else from the book, learn this. It starts with relationships, and those relationships exist when you deliver a podcast of *value*. If you picked up this book to get rich quick, put it down now. If you picked up this book because you just *had* to create a podcast about your subject and would talk about it for free—but would prefer not to—then read on. It all boils down to delivering value, serving your audience, and developing relationships. I'm going to say that again.

> *It all boils down to delivering value, serving your audience, and developing relationships.*

This book is about making money with your podcast. Well, that's not entirely true. Your podcast is how you distribute your message. What will motive people into action is the *relationship* you build with your audience. You build that *relationship* by delivering phenomenal content (via your podcast) and by responding to emails, voice mails, and comments.

Relationships built on interaction are nothing new. Marketing has always involved knowing your target market and developing relationships. This book is about making money with your *relationship* that grows by delivering *valuable* podcasts episodes that inspire the listener to tell their friends.

PODCASTING BENEFITS

Podcasting's benefits come in different forms. Here are just a few:

- You will be an expert (if you feel like one or not).
- You can keep your name/brand in front of potential customers.

- You can increase sales of products or services.
- You gain an understanding of your market (through feedback).
- You gain trust in the eyes of potential customers.
- You reach a global audience.

These are just a handful of benefits. Here are some examples of how engaged audiences have been moved to action by their relationships with podcasters:

1. Hall of Fame podcaster Adam Curry and John C. Dvorak produce the *No Agenda Show* (noagendashow.com). They have people join their "Knight" program by donating $1,000 or more. They are adding more and more Knights (and Dames for females) daily. Their show delivers (in an entertaining way) information that is missing in the mainstream media (but should be included).

2. Hall of Fame podcasters Keith Malley and Chemda from *Keith and The Girl* (www.katg.com) have such rabid fans that they have gone from having the *Keith and The Girl* logo tattooed on their bodies to having the logo *branded* on their bodies. These fans also purchase their comedy books and CDs. Their book, *What Do We Do Now?: Keith and The Girl's Smart Answers to Your Stupid Relationship Questions,* made it to #35 in their category on Amazon.com. Keith is a comedian who sells out his shows and is featured on SiriusXM satellite radio. The duo has appeared in the *New York Times*, the *Wall Street Journal,* and many other publications.

3. Hall of Fame podcaster Scott Sigler (www.scottsigler.com) could not get a publisher to take a chance on his books featuring a mix of sci-fi and horror. He decided to give away his entire book for free via his podcast. His listeners had already consumed his book and loved it. When he published a print version of his book *Infected*, his fans showed their support by buying the book (that they had previously received free) and it shot up to #2 on Amazon.com. The book would have been #1 on all of Amazon except for a book about a kid named Harry Potter. See https://youtu.be/Yg-EMvPhh9A.

4. Dr. Emily Morse started the *Sex with Emily* podcast in 2005 and was featured in the Apple Podcasts directory (sexwithemily .com). Her endless popularity in the Apple directory caught the attention of radio executives in San Francisco and led to her taking her podcast to the FM airwaves (until they changed their format). She hosted the *Miss Advised* show on the Bravo Network on television. She frequently contributes to major publications, such as *Cosmopolitan, Glamour, New York Magazine, Bustle, Ask Men, Elite Daily, Men's Health, and Harper's Bazaar.* Emily can be seen as a guest on TV programs like *The Today Show, Entertainment Tonight, E! and The Doctors.* Networks including NBC, CBS, ABC, and HLN have turned to Emily to serve as their sex and relationship expert on a variety of segments and specials. While radio and TV shows have come and gone, one thing has stayed consistent: she continues to do her podcast and maintain that relationship with her audience. She is currently featured on SiriusXM.

5. John Dennis created the *Smart Time Online* show that still brings him leads. He had to pause the podcast as it brought him too many clients. When I interviewed him, he said, "I got a Fortune 500 multibillion-dollar client out of my podcast. One of the digital heads for this company heard my show and then heard me speak about a subject where they needed help. She came to listen to me speak as a result of hearing my show." A conversation ensued, which led to a contract.

6. Michael Butler is the host of the *Rock and Roll Geek* show (rockandrollgeek.com). He was able to interview one of his all-time favorite musicians on his podcast. Later, this musician asked him to play bass in his band at a special event in London. Michael's audience paid for his trip from the United States to London, where Michael stayed for free with listeners (and played bass with one of his favorite musicians).

7. When Oprah Winfrey wanted to do a show about grammar, the name that came up was *Grammar Girl*, who is better known as Mignon Fogarty. Oprah's producers were aware of Mignon due to her *Grammar Girl* podcast. She quickly took some of her episodes and turned it into a book. She went on to form the Quick and Dirty Tips network (quickanddirtytips.

com), and if you search for her name in Amazon, you will see she has many books and calendars, with some of them translated into different languages.

8. Chris Christensen produces the *Amateur Traveler* podcast, where he occasionally receives free trips to exotic locations so he can review them for his audience. Chris also sells photographs that he takes at these locations.

9. John Lee Dumas produces the *Entrepreneurs on Fire* podcast (eofire.com). John lists his income reports on his website (www.eofire.com/income). In January 2018, John's show made $205,842. We will talk more about John a little later. Just be clear, that amount is what he made *in a month*. (Source: www.eofire.com/income53)

10. Gary Leland previously spent $100,000 on Google AdWords when he first started his podcast. Gary has a sporting goods store and created a podcast around women's fast pitch softball (fastpitchradio.com). He is the sponsor of his show and creates the podcast his target audience wants to hear. Now Gary no longer needs to advertise on Google, and that $100,000 goes right to the bottom line.

11. Pat Flynn started a blog in 2008. It was hugely successful and helped launch his first business. In 2010 he started the *Smart Passive Income* podcast. When I met him at an event, he told me how everyone at the podcasting event was saying, "Pat, I love your podcast," but nobody seemed to comment on his blog. He already had a very engaged audience from his blog, but that engagement increased with his podcast. Pat has been making five- and six-figure *monthly* incomes ever since (I consider him the king of affiliate marketing), and like every other successful podcaster he created products after learning the needs of his audience. When I went to smartpassiveincome.com in 2019, it showed his income for the previous twelve months was $2,171,652.55.

These are just a few examples of podcast success. As you can see, you don't always get paid in cash, but there are many benefits from podcasting. I have twice achieved full-time employment because of my knowledge of podcasting. I have received products for free and been asked to speak at conventions.

I have been on the radio and television. I have interviewed my heroes. I have received donations from listeners. Seventy percent of the people who sign up for my membership site (schoolofpodcasting.com) use a coupon that is only available by listening to the podcast. The point is, you can make money with a podcast. With the right combination of determination mixed with phenomenal content, promotion, and production, you can build a successful podcast.

WHAT THIS BOOK IS AND WHAT THIS BOOK IS NOT

This book assumes that you have a podcast. I assume that you are using WordPress to manage your website. Why WordPress? It is free, powerful, and easy to use. When I go to podcast conferences, everyone I talk to is using WordPress. According to venturebeat.com, currently, about 30 percent of the Internet runs on WordPress. Please note, I said managing your *website* with WordPress. I recommend that you manage your podcast feed with your media host. You can use Squarespace and other platforms, but I will be mentioning many things that are WordPress specific.

This book will *not* show you how to record a podcast. What this book *is* about are the tips and tricks podcasters have used to make money with podcasting. I will also give you some tips and useful resources. I'm also assuming your show is good, and by this, I mean someone not named Mom has told you it's good.

THE POWER OF THE NICHE EXPLAINED

When I say "Never underestimate the power of the niche," what do I mean? Let's look at an example. Let's say you do a podcast for triathletes. Someone who has a product for that niche can advertise on the radio, but only 5 percent of the radio audience is their target market. Now your podcast comes along, and your audience is 100 percent triathletes. Where would you spend your advertising dollars if you were that company? The radio station may have a larger audience, but the podcast has a higher quality of listener.

THE PROFIT FROM YOUR PODCAST COMPANION COURSE

I know what you're thinking: *Oh, I knew there would be a catch!* But this isn't an "AHA!" moment. I'm not trying to sell you some additional course. In fact, it is free (for you) as my way of saying thank you for buying the book. I'm a teacher at heart, and some things are easier to understand via audio and video, instead of words on a page. If you've made it this far, I appreciate you making the effort and I will have bonus content, resources, etc. at www .profitfromyourpodcast.com/bonus. I'm not going to make it too difficult to join this, so let's keep this link between you and me. Okay?

SUMMARY

- Podcasting is a great tool to help build relationships with your audience and increases your chances of being an expert in your niche.
- This book will provide tips on tools to use and strategies for making money.
- While a niche audience is smaller in numbers, it will be engaging and loyal.
- There are benefits from podcasting in addition to money.

2

Get an Audience

FIRST THINGS FIRST—WHO IS YOUR AUDIENCE AND DO THEY HAVE ANY MONEY?

You need to know your audience. If you don't know your listeners, how will you know what to give them? Another thing you might want to think about is if they have a budget. The more you "guess" at these answers (I *think* they have a budget), the bigger the risk you are wasting your time.

I did a podcast for musicians. You know all those jokes about "starving artists"—well, it's not a joke. At one point, I put my book on sale for .99, and I didn't get a sale. These people had no budget. I did that podcast for ten years and probably had one sale a year. However, I did it for fun. I got to talk to my musical heroes. My point here is that the audience was broke.

Daniel J. Lewis has a background in web design. His websites look *great*. His podcast is called *The Audacity to Podcast* (theaudacitytopodcast.com), as in "Do you have the courage (audacity) to podcast?" There is also a free software used by *many* podcasters called (you guessed it) Audacity. Daniel inherited a ton of website visitors who thought his podcast was all about Audacity. These people like Audacity because it's *free*. Let's say it was safe to say that the audience that was willing to pay zero for their software was not willing to pay four figures for their web design.

Daniel also discovered, when he sold an online workshop on how to use Audacity, that people who love the free software are not thrilled to spend money to learn how to use it. Don't feel bad for Daniel; you'll hear more about him later.

NO AUDIENCE—NO MONEY

These tips may not always directly relate to making money. What they do is give you insights into what makes a great podcast. Great podcasts inspire their audience to tell their friends and have a much better chance of making money. Remember, the first step of making money with a podcast is to build an audience. You build an audience by creating content that inspires others to tell their friends.

CONTENT IS KING

You will hear this again and again. Content is KING. If you want people to tune in, then your content must be phenomenal.

Too many people are asking, "How do I make money?" before they ask, "How do I make great content?" I can't stress this enough. Your audience will give value (money) for valuable content.

Podcasting is about building relationships. Without good content, your audience will not come back. Without repeat consumers, a relationship will not thrive. Without the relationship, there will be little (if any) money.

What is great content? To answer this, I reverse-engineered any media I consumed. Here is what I found:

- It's content that moves you.
- It taps into your emotions.
- It entertains you.
- It makes you laugh.
- It makes you cry.
- It makes you think.
- It makes you groan.
- It educates or entertains you.

If you can either help people or entertain them, you are on the right track. If you can do both, you have stumbled upon what can be a very magic formula.

When I think of the television shows I consume, they all hit me emotionally. They move and inspire me. Even if they inspire me to throw things at the screen, they move me. The next time you find yourself sitting in your driveway listening to a podcast instead of getting out of the car and going into the house, you are consuming phenomenal content.

Hall of Fame Podcaster Dan Klass does a podcast which features stories about his life as a father, actor, and comedian called *The Bitterest Pill* (thebitterestpill.com). On more than one occasion, I have driven home only to sit in my driveway listening to the end of the story in my car.

That's great content that moves me.

The great thing about podcasting is you have the same global reach that can touch the same number of people as a giant network. In the early days of podcasting, Dave Swerdlick and his two daughters produced the *Kid Friday* podcast. This podcast was created in their basement and yet routinely topped other podcasts that were created by Nickelodeon, Universal Studios, and Disney. What does the Swerdlick family have? They have great content.

When I spoke with Dr. Emily Morse of *Sex with Emily*, she said one sponsor saw a 40 percent spike in sales when she mentioned a specific product on her podcast.

I interviewed Kathy and Steve Elkins, who own WEBS (a knitting and crochet retailer), back in 2012. You can find them at yarn.com. They also produce a podcast on knitting. After producing 208 episodes, they had about 13,000 listeners per week (remember, this was back in 2012), and the results were evident in the company's sales. Just like Emily, they mentioned a product on their show and saw a spike in sales of that item.

What made it successful? Kathy Elkins cites promoting the podcast on the company's other social media channels, keeping content interesting, sticking to a schedule, and not using the podcast as a commercial. "It's like inviting people into the shop and having a cup of tea, and it's the same conversation I would have as if I were sitting there knitting with them."

They are building a relationship. They are educating people on their products. They provide great content for a specific niche.

In some cases, your best content will come from your audience. When Glenn Hebert launched his daily *Horses in the Morning* show, his most popular (now sponsored) segment didn't exist. His audience started sending in really bad ads from people selling their horses on Craigslist. As he started reading these ads, more people started to send them in. They got so many (hundreds per week) that they made "Really Bad Ads" a segment that they saved for the last half hour of their Friday show. They get double the listeners for just the "Really Bad Ads" segment. When I asked Glenn how he grows his audience, he gave me a great three-word answer: "Don't be boring." The "Really Bad Ads" segment is two things. It's entertaining (I am not a horse person, but I tune in on Fridays to listen), and it's educational (as you learn what *not* to do in your advertisement). You can hear Glenn at horseradionetwork.com.

YOUR GOAL IS NOT THE APPLE CHARTS

What does appearing on the Apple charts mean? When I first started studying podcast monetization for the people who produce the *How Stuff Works* podcast, it meant about 3.8 million downloads in November 2010. *Kevin Pollak's Chat Show* (an Apple charts regular) had 1.2 million downloads in December 2010. How did they do it? They had great content. I know you're going to say, "But Kevin Pollak is a famous actor and comedian." To this I say, "The Swerdlick family is not." Their success proves that any dad and his two daughters *with great content* can top the charts.

Now, with over 870,000 podcasts in the Apple Podcasts directory, getting up the charts doesn't give you as much (if any) of a boost. Some podcasters obsess over being "featured" in New and Noteworthy (a special area in the Apple Podcasts app), but I've known people who have been in that section, and it brought a whopping thirty-two extra downloads. I've known podcasters who have been on the FRONT PAGE of Apple Podcasts and got a few hundred (not thousand) downloads in a week.

I include this brief history of Apple because many people *still* think that getting into Apple is all you need to do (it's not). They've probably read an old blog post from 2012 (or earlier). Podcast directories are a phone book. Being in the phone book does not make you famous. It's a nice place that makes it easier to be found. However, with 870,000 podcasts in Apple Podcasts, being found can be quite a challenge (see my video that explains this more at https://youtu.be/uTIrfG3gDvc). If your marketing plan is "Get into Apple," you need to go back to the drawing board—as well as realize that 80 percent of Europe uses an Android phone.

When I hear the phrase "New and Noteworthy," I throw up in my mouth (just a little bit) as people *obsess* over this area of Apple. Again, this does not provide instant stardom. Focus on your audience, and you will end up in New and Noteworthy. Instead, people focus on New and Noteworthy and hope it builds their audience.

Staring at your downloads stats does not make them grow.

People get hung up on hardware and on making their podcasts have pristine sound quality while spending less time on creating good content. To me, this is like swinging your dull axe harder when chopping down a tree. I prefer to sharpen my axe. Great content helps you cut through the crowd and stand out. The key to your audio quality is it can't be distracting. If your audio is not distracting (with lots of reverb and room noise), then quit shopping for microphones and get back to making great content.

Tim Ferriss (tim.blog) has the *Tim Ferriss Show* (which has over 400 million downloads), which according to an image on his Instagram is recorded on his kitchen island with a seventy-dollar microphone and a five-dollar windscreen (www.instagram.com/p/B0gknQuH7Kx/).

CONTENT DOESN'T GROW ON TREES

In researching people who are having success in podcasting, I noticed a trait. They did things that other people didn't.

Jordan Harbinger of *The Jordan Harbinger Show* (jordanharbinger.com) does the work. If he interviews an author, he reads their book before the interview. He does a TON of research, so he knows the answers before he even asks the question. When I listen to his show, I hear guests say things like, "Wow, that's a really good question" (and mean it) or "Wow, I haven't talked about this in years." I listened to his episode where he interviewed the late Kobe Bryant, and within the first few minutes, Jordan was asking him about his writing. Jordan said, "Well, you got interested in writing in high school." This question is the ultimate "Jordan-ism." You know immediately that this guy has done a TON of homework on his subject. Who knew Kobe Bryant was interested in writing in high school? Jordan went on to talk about so many subjects with Kobe. It was so different than any other Kobe Bryant interview. Did I share it on social? You bet I did, and I told my friends, "Jordan got to interview Kobe Bryant." Jordan addresses how he was able to get Kobe on his show. What is his secret? *Relationships* (Jordan has a free course on networking). As of this writing Jordan has 250,000 downloads per episode (and climbing). As I said, Jordan does the work, and it shows.

When I interviewed Pat Flynn, he explained that in the early days of his blog (smartpassiveincome.com) he wrote his posts so specific that a reader could pass a test about the subject. Adding these details would often take more than an hour. It was those posts that had people linking to them, which helped him be found by Google, which led to more sales.

Paula Pant of *Afford Anything* (affordanything.com) has stated that if she is interviewing an author, she may spend ten hours doing research, reading the book, etc., to prepare for the interview. Her episodes get mid-five-figure downloads per episode. Are you noticing a pattern?

Liz Covart of *Ben Franklin's World* (benfranklinsworld.com) spends AN HOUR per minute of her show. If your brain is having a hard time doing the math, a fifteen-minute show will take her fifteen hours.

Does this mean you can't scan someone's bio, listen to five minutes of a podcast, and do an interview? You can, but who is going to ask the better questions? Who understands their guest better and can steer their answers in a way to provide value for their audience? Some create a podcast as a hobby. They do it to talk to interesting people. If you are running your podcast as a business, you must do those things that other podcasters don't. Radio host (and podcaster, author, speaker) Dave Ramsey has a saying: "If you live like no one else, later you can live like no one else." If we tweak this a bit, if you podcast like no one else, later you will have an audience like no one else.

Don't confuse activity with busy. Some people spend *hours* creating content. That time spent is because they did not prepare and are trying to fix things later with editing. When people ask me how to cut down the amount of time they spend editing, I always ask them how much preparation they did. My record for the number of times I've re-recorded an episode was four. Why? Because I had the content in my head and told myself, "I know what I want to say." I turned on the microphone and let it rip. Each time I would take a mental tangent, and eventually hit stop and think, *How did I end up here?* Eventually, I took the five minutes to write out a few bullet points to keep me focused. The fourth recording was focused and on point. The more planning, the less editing. My father used to tell me, "Measure twice, cut once."

In the same way that reality TV has very little reality in it, setting up a few microphones and having chitchat is not what successful podcasters are doing.

DON'T DO THIS

I was listening to a show that looks at old movies and such from the 1980s. Ann asked Duane if he had watched the movie (these names have been changed to protect the stupid). The answer? No, Duane had not. Ann moved forward talking about the movie that Duane had not watched. I am not making this up.

I once pressed play and heard, "So do you want to talk about the story in the *Times* or the *Tribune*?" They went back and forth on the subjects. Determining what to talk about is not a bad discussion to have *before* you press record.

Don't announce your transition. "Hey, Susan, do you want to go to the lightning round?" JUST GO TO THE LIGHTNING ROUND.

I could provide hundreds of examples, but the one that truly blows me away was a sports podcast that pulls clips to promote the radio show of the host. The well-produced intro comes on announcing the host, and the host does a nice job of introducing this famous catcher in baseball. He asks the first question, and the microphone isn't on. The host says, "Hold on a second, the microphone isn't on," and they fix it. My thought is this: You have hours of a broadcast to pick from, and you choose to leave in the technical difficulties, when you could easily edit them out? *THIS* is your *BEST* clip of the day?

Okay, one more. You may feel brave. It may sound fun. But getting drunk with your friend and recording your conversation very rarely produces any valuable content. Keep in mind this might be the top result when your future boss googles your name.

DO THINGS THAT BIGGER SHOWS CAN'T

In Pat Flynn's book *Superfans,* he mentions how he would grab ten random emails from people who recently joined his email list and ask if they can get on the phone and have a quick chat. I call this fanning the flames. These people have already taken a step further to know you (signing up for your newsletter), and now when they get the chance to talk to you, they are getting off the phone and telling someone (if not everyone) they know.

I use a tool called Vidyard (vidyard.com) to record and send quick video emails to people who sign up at the School of Podcasting. People always think it's some premade cookie-cutter generic auto responder. Then they click play and hear me say their name. They can't believe it. These videos don't take long (a few minutes apiece), and the results are amazing. I also use these to answer questions from potential clients (as well as existing clients). I can also see when someone has watched the video.

If you don't have the budget for some of these tools, instead of staring at your download stats, stare at your audience. You need to answer every email, tweet, mention, etc. You want to fan the flames.

One of the reasons I do this is because HUGE podcasts can't. Even though they may have a staff of eighteen, they can't personally welcome everyone—but you can. Embrace your "smallness" when you first start and do those things that bigger shows can't.

GIVE YOUR AUDIENCE SOMETHING TO TALK ABOUT

In the fitness industry, almost every weight loss plan begins with a "quick start" (often some cleanse). Why? Because the person can see it start to work quickly. Amazed, they will start to tell their friends. Quickly, they are developing faith in the diet plan and develop the courage to keep on going.

Your podcast is the same way. When I give someone a strategy, a technique, and it works, they trust the words coming out of my mouth. They also tell a friend about it.

Don't worry about "giving away the farm." Some people use the rule of, "I will tell you *what* to do for free, and I will charge you for the *how to do it steps*." I understand that, but I still will occasionally tell my audience how to do something. Why? Because Mike Russell of Music Radio Creative (musicradiocreative.com) is an Adobe ninja. When I watch his YouTube channel, and he does magical things in the Adobe Audition software, it looks easy. Then when I try it, I realize I don't have the years of audio editing at this deeper level that Mike does. Consequently, if I want it done at that level, I will hire Mike (and often do).

People pay for free things all the time. Don't believe me? You can watch the movie the *Wizard of Oz* on television regularly (and if it's on TBS you'll get commercials that feel like they appear every ten minutes). The movie is available on Amazon as a DVD anytime you want it. People will pay for things they can get for free. While my content may be available for free scattered among hundreds of blog posts and podcast episodes, you can pay to have it all organized in one place by joining my membership site.

HOW TO GROW YOUR AUDIENCE

Growing your audience is one of those topics where people ask questions, but often won't take the steps to make it happen. Here they are:

1. Figure out who your target audience is. "Everybody" is not an acceptable answer.
2. Determine what they want to hear.
3. Create content that will deliver value and inspire them to tell a friend.
4. Get someone not named Mom to review your show. Preferably a target audience member. Start a Facebook group and give them a link to your episode (share it in dropbox.com or other media sharing service). Then ask them to "Talk about the podcast like I'm not in the room." You can give them a survey to fill out, but if you can explain how you TRULY want to make

this the best show ever, and that you can handle some constructive feedback, you can get some people to provide feedback. Many people aren't willing to take feedback.

   a. Did you know that the original captain in the original *Star Trek* series was not Captain Kirk? It also wasn't William Shatner. The show's producers got a focus group and tweaked things. Fifty-four years later, I'd say the feedback helped.

   b. Failure to skip this step can cost tons of money spent on advertising that only alerts the rest of the world that your show is boring sooner than later.

5. Go to where the audience is. Locations might be Facebook groups, meetup.com, events, etc. When you can see your audience's eye color, that is the best. Seeing them face-to-face may require you to get out of your chair. These steps can be too much of a hurdle for some people.

6. Make friends with them and *bring value* to every conversation. Also, listen to the conversations that are happening (as these may be topics for future episodes).

7. Tell them about your show.

8. Repeat steps 1–7.

I know this sounds too simple, but in a nutshell, that is how you grow your audience, and here is why.

I once found a forum (this was before Facebook) of ex-radio people. I thought I heard angels singing when it came up in my search results. This was the mother lode, I thought. These were people who probably wanted to get back in front of an audience, knew their way around a microphone, but didn't understand how to start a podcast. This forum truly was a pot of gold.

My first post was something along the lines of "Hey, everybody, I'm Dave Jackson from the School of Podcasting. I've been podcasting since 2005, and if you want to get your voice heard, I've started a website to teach people how to podcast at www.schoolofpodcasting.com."

I was so excited. I went in guns a-blazin'. I thought I was going to be their hero.

I was banned from the group in less than ten minutes. My pot of gold was forever out of my reach.

The moral of this story is nobody knows you, and nobody wants to know you until you give them a reason to care. I know that sounds harsh (and it is), but it's true. I don't care that you walked to school both ways uphill in a snowstorm. I don't care until you can do something for me. THEN I will be interested in your backstory.

There is a line in podcasting and radio circles that your station is WIFM (what's in it for me).

Remember, step six is to go and make friends. Step seven is to tell them about your show. Do not swap these two steps.

NEVER LOSE THEIR TRUST

One thing that EVERY podcaster starts with when they launch a podcast is integrity. Hopefully, years later, when you look back you still have it.

While you don't *have* to be consistent when you publish a podcast, it helps. Why? Because you become part of their routine. You become trusted. I have released an episode of the School of Podcasting every Monday for over fifteen years. I once totaled my car when a deer jumped on the hood. I always travel with a laptop and a microphone, so I produced an episode in the hotel.

Consequently, I have people say things like, "You're with me every Monday when I take the kids to school," or "You're with me on the way to the feed store." One person said I was with them in the shower every Monday. I'm not sure how I feel about that.

When I was in my twenties, I was training people on how to run their office equipment. I would ask when the best time would be to check up on the account. They might answer to call in the afternoon in two weeks. I would then call in two weeks in the afternoon, and I always found it odd that people would be AMAZED that I had called. All I was doing was sticking to my word. I told them I would call in two weeks, and I did. Keeping your word can go a long way in podcasting.

I saw this firsthand with my *Marketing Musician* podcast. I had lost my passion after producing it for eleven years. I would skip a week here or there and not alert my audience ahead of time. My episodes weren't as good. I saw my numbers start to dwindle. I started to see less engagement. The ultimate sign that the show had lost its audience was when I released part one of an interview. I skipped the next week with no explanation. Not a single person has ever asked me, "Where is part two?" as I never released another episode of that show.

Your audience likes you. They want the best for you. If you're going to take a break, let them know when you will be leaving and when you should be returning. Your audience will understand. Mike Rowe of *The Way I Heard It* podcast took some time off to write a book. He explained when he would be back. He explained he could write a book, or he could record a podcast, but he couldn't do both. I like Mike. I had no problem with that and looked forward to the day I could buy his book. When Mike came back on the date he said he would, he had an announcement. His podcast was being turned into a TV show.

GROWING YOUR AUDIENCE WITH A PARTNER

One strategy for monetization and for growing your audience is to approach monetization by looking beyond sponsorship and looking for a partner. What is a partner? A partner is someone who not only pays you with money, but they also help promote your podcast.

Lee Silverstein—*We Have Cancer*

In the case of Lee Silverstein of the *We Have Cancer* podcast (wehavecancer-show.com), Lee said, "Instead of asking whose product can I help sell, I went looking for someone's message that I can help magnify." Lee aligned his podcast with a large nonprofit cancer organization. He explained that they occasionally would provide a guest, and they retweet all his episode mentions.

Someone who listens to Lee's show may get inspired to help the cause and then donate to the nonprofit. The nonprofit benefits, the audience benefits through great content, and Lee benefits through sponsorship and by helping his community.

It wasn't always easy. When Lee approached his first organization, they didn't want to participate. They would later contact Lee and ask to get involved. Why? Because they heard other people talking about his show (as I said, make content that inspires people to tell their friends). If you receive a "No," realize it may be a "Not now" and not a "Never."

For me, when you get a "No," use the attitude that comedian Kevin Hart mentions in his book *I Can't Make This Up*. When Kevin would get rejected, he would say to himself, "I'm going to work on my act and be so funny that they won't be able to say no in the future."

Lee has had stage four colon cancer for *years*, so you don't have to worry about Lee giving up. Lee has had sponsors in the past that included products that were directly related to cancer patients. His current partnership with the nonprofit is more consistent and benefits everyone involved.

Liz Covart—*Ben Franklin's World*

Historian Liz Covart started her show *Ben Franklin's World* (benfranklinsworld.com) as a hobby, and it took off. She reached out to fellow historian Karin Wulf, who had mentioned the "business side of history" during a talk, for some advice. As Liz put it, "I didn't know there was a business side of history." Karin brought Liz out to the Omohundro Institute of Early American History and Culture at William and Mary, where institute staff walked Liz through the publishing process for academic book reviews (as this seemed to be the closest analogy for her podcast work).

Liz mentioned that her audience had been asking about how historians work (please note that Liz was giving her audience what they wanted), and the Omohundro Institute (OI) offered to partner with her to produce a series on that topic. The OI paid to produce fourteen episodes. The partnership proved successful, as it brought attention to the organization and shined a spotlight on the work of historians.

The OI was very eager to start season two. However, as it often happens, Liz had underestimated the work it took to produce the episodes and asked for more money to produce a second season. Rather than pay Liz as a contractor, the OI created a job for her as its digital projects editor. They also agreed to supply Liz with a team to help produce the podcast and to help with marketing and promotion.

What started as a hobby about history ended up as a job in academia. Here again, we see a partnership where both parties win.

Doug Parsons—*America Adapts: The Climate Change Podcast*

Doug Parsons hosts and produces *America Adapts: The Climate Change Podcast* (americaadapts.org). He has been doing the show for three years. After his first year, he wanted to take it more seriously and investigated becoming a 501(c)(3) nonprofit. In looking into this model, there were many hurdles (including forming a board) and other items that seemed out of reach for someone just starting.

Doug started researching fiscal sponsors. Fiscal sponsors are organizations that already have nonprofit status and can take other organizations (like Doug's) under their umbrella. Fiscal sponsors take 6 to 10 percent of your charitable donations (which is less than some crowdfunding tools—and the donations are tax deductible for our audience).

Doug ended up with the Social Good Fund (www.socialgoodfund.org), who have a mission "to create and establish positive influences for individuals, communities, and the environment. Our goal is to sponsor and develop projects that will help positively impact and develop local communities into healthier and happier places to live, work, and be." They offer back-office support, human resources, bookkeeping, coaching, and tools to make it easy to accept donations.

One of the advantages of this situation is Doug always has immediate access to his funds with a project expense card. They have a great page that makes it easy to donate at americaadapts.wedid.it, which can be a one-time donation or can be set up to be recurring.

Doug has been approached by other climate-related companies who then partner/sponsor episodes on Doug's podcast. Here again, the featured company gets exposure in front of Doug's audience. These companies are primarily looking for exposure and to get the word out (there isn't much of a call to action). Doug gets content that relates to his audience, and he gets compensated for putting their content in front of his audience. I will come back to this idea later as it is a common thread among podcasters.

Doug is finding sponsors this way but faces the challenges that all podcasters face. Many companies don't understand the power of podcasting. He often suggests that instead of spending thousands of dollars on writing a report that nobody will see or read (not an exaggeration), take that money and put that content out as a podcast in front of an already established audience.

While fiscal sponsorship may only work for a small number of podcasters, if you're podcasting for a cause, you may want to investigate a fiscal sponsor.

Glenn Hebert—Horse Radio Network

You are going to hear about Glenn Hebert a lot in this book because he's a genius. He runs the Horse Radio Network (www.horseradionetwork.com). He has been on my *School of Podcasting* show more than any other guest. He started his network with one show. For a while, he would say his only show was part of a network (but had the vision to know his one show would someday be one of many). He now has sixteen-plus shows and has recorded thousands of episodes. Glenn "gets it." He is ALWAYS building relationships. Here is a genius example of how Glenn grows his audience through partnerships.

There was a HUGE horse show that was not open to the public. Glenn approached the show and asked to be the "official radio network" of their show. He said, "All you need to do is give us a booth for free. We will pay our way, and we will do a radio show from your event. We will get some of the manufacturers on the show to promote their products [which makes it easy for the event to sell booths if one of the perks is you might be on a podcast for horse owners], and we will promote your event." They said yes (why wouldn't they?).

In the early days, Glenn said they would give him the leftover booths. Years later, he now gets a prime spot and on his LIVE (more on that when we talk tools) show on Monday morning he has fifteen manufacturers do a quick three-minute spot to talk about their latest products (especially any new products Glenn's audience hasn't heard about). The first few years Glenn had to do some explaining to manufacturers on what it was he was doing (a radio what? A pod what?). Now the manufacturers are asking Glenn to be on his show and leaving "I want to be on your show" notes for him at his booth.

What do these little three-minute segments do? It is the beginning of a *relationship* with a potential sponsor for Glenn's show. When the manufacturer discovers that Glenn has an audience of "horse people," they don't stay a *potential* sponsor for long, as they want to get their products in front of Glenn's audience. Seventy percent of his sponsors come from that show, and 70 percent of them remain sponsors. We will talk more about how Glenn handles sponsorships and how he PARTNERS with his sponsors later in the book.

This "get a booth" strategy has now made Glenn a verb. When people tell me that they heard Glenn on my show and that they will have a booth at a trade show in their niche, they contact me and say, "I Glenn the Geeked it."

One other side of the strategy is when you do a show that is open to the public. There will often be speakers, attendees, and sponsors. We've already heard how partnering with sponsors is a great strategy, but interviewing the speakers grows your network, and those interviews provide more great content (for more information on doing interviews see www.schoolofpodcasting .com/677), but going to an event for the public gets you in front of your target audience. THIS IS HUGE.

When I have someone walk up to me and say, "Hey Dave, I listen to your show and love it," I STOP WHATEVER I'M DOING AND GIVE THEM MY UNDIVIDED ATTENTION. I ask them why they love it, and I bring some extra skin and ask them if there is anything they would change. Then shut up. By that, I mean don't say anything. They will be polite and say, "I wouldn't change a thing." That's fine and nice to hear. Create an awkward pause (it's harder than it sounds), and typically they may mention something that they might change. Seventy percent of podcasts (according to Jacobs Media) grow by word of mouth, and you have your target audience in front of you. Take advantage of it and get some feedback.

Lastly, don't let them leave without taking a selfie. Why? One, they may be too nervous to ask you for one, and two, what are they going to do with a selfie? They are going to post it on social media and talk about how they met *you* from (the name of your show). Nothing is more important than your audience.

Nothing.

3

Presentation Is Queen

If your content is King, then your presentation is Queen. What is presentation? To me, presentation includes:

- The look and feel of your website
- The quality of your audio/video
- The flow of the content in your episodes

How does this tie into making money? I was approved to have a trial product sent to me based on the sponsor's first impression of my website. It loaded fast, had good graphics, and wasn't too cluttered. Many times, we want everything to be on the front page. We end up putting so much on the front page that you can't find anything. It's a giant pile of clutter. You need to identify your top priority. If you are trying to build an email list, put the email sign-up box on the front page. If you are trying to get subscribers, put links to subscribe on the front page. If you want to feature an advertiser, put that on the front page. However, all these items can't fit on the front page "above the fold" (a term from the newspaper industry, which means the part of your website that people do not have to scroll to see). With multiple options, you need to decide on your main call to action.

I also recommend making sure that when you add ID3 tags to your media (audio or video), there is an image used. This way, when it plays on a few apps, a picture will display. ID3 tagging is all part of your branding and makes you look professional. If you are using a PC, check out MP3TAG. ID3 Editor works on both Macs and PCs. ID3 tags aren't as important as when I first wrote this book, but they take all of ten seconds to add to your file.

Your production is also important. I once found a podcast with a topic that was custom-made for my interest. However, the audio sounded like someone was frying bacon underwater. It had massive volume changes, and you could barely understand what the person was saying due to background noise. You also need to remember that your audience may be in a car doing sixty miles per hour (which creates some noise). I didn't even make it through the first episode and never gave them a second chance. If you are doing a podcast with more than one person, and your volume levels differ, test-drive a free service at auphonic.com (it adjusts volumes levels and removes noise). If I am forced to adjust my volume knob as I listen, your production needs improvement.

I once had a guest who was in an RV in the desert. She didn't turn off her air conditioning, and it made for a horrible recording. I used some fancy expensive software to clean up a lot of the background noise, but in the end, one listener named John left this comment on the post: *"Dave, interesting guest but audio quality is not acceptable. Don't know why or if you can control this problem. She sounds like she's talking into an empty coffee can. Unfortunate for her and you. Enjoy your show. Thanks."*

The flow of your content is also part of the presentation. You should realize that we live in a society where people's attention is their most prized possession. I once listened to a podcast that took *seventeen minutes* to get to the main topic. What did I have to sit through? I heard how the host hated Bob Seger music. They rambled on how their kids had been driving them crazy, etc. None of these topics had anything to do with the podcast (and wasted my time). GET TO THE POINT. You don't hear a newscast start with, "Our top story today is coming up in about twenty minutes."

While people enjoy getting to know the host, watch out that the "witty banter" doesn't take up 30 percent of the show. You might also do it at the end of the show (after the main topic). People know what they want, and they want it now. Nobody complains about not getting to the point. The bottom line is that I never listened to another episode of this podcast. If your witty banter can include the topic of the show, then you're on the right track. Now not only are you revealing a personal story, but you are staying on topic.

If you don't believe me when I say people want you to get to the point, then watch something on Netflix. There is the option to "skip intro" when the video starts. At the end, if it is a series, and you click "skip outro," not only does it skip the outro it also skips the intro of the next episode, getting you to the content even quicker.

In 2019 Google announced that podcast episodes would start appearing in search results. Podcasts in search results mean if someone googles the phrase "NASCAR podcast" and finds your show, they expect to hear you talk about NASCAR quickly (and not "How is the weather?").

IS YOUR PODCAST ADVERTISER FRIENDLY?

Now, I'm not saying you don't have a right to be over the top and say all the "naughty" words that will make your mother gasp. You have the right to go right ahead and say them, but don't complain when Howard Stern is famous and you're not. It takes more than the "seven dirty words" to build an audience.

If you listen to Howard Stern, you realize there is more there than fart jokes. Howard Stern was one of the first to understand that it was about creating a relationship with the audience, by providing content they couldn't get anywhere else (his life, behind the scenes of the radio business). While many people think he's just about penis jokes, Howard chooses not to judge. Instead of judging the prostitute, he interviewed her and asked her all the questions that you want to ask a prostitute. It was content you couldn't get anywhere else.

Did Howard recently ask Hall of Fame football player Joe Namath if he has enough sex? Yep. It was also obvious that Howard had done a ton of preparation for this interview. Talk to any guest after their appearance on Howard's show, and they will talk about the relationship they feel with Howard during the interview—how he makes them feel calm and as if it is just the two of them talking (when there are really millions listening in). So here again, it's all about the preparation and the *relationship*.

In his movie *Howard Stern's Private Parts,* there is a scene that states the top reason fans listen to Howard Stern is: *they don't know what they are going to hear next.* One of the top reasons people HATE Howard Stern is: *they don't know what they are going to hear next.*

If all you do is make jokes about 9/11 victims, abortions, and people with AIDS, you will be predictable. It takes more than seven dirty words and a lack of tact.

This isn't to say that you can't find advertisers with an "adult"-oriented podcast. There are adult sites such as Adam & Eve, Good Vibrations, Ashley Madison, and others that have sponsored shows in the past. Dr. Emily Morse of the *Sex with Emily* show (sexwithemily.com) has been talking about "adult" topics since 2005. Just realize there is a difference between *Sex with Emily* and *Cum Town* (shoutengine.com/CumTown/), which features comedians.

However, don't feel bad for *Cum Town*; the last time I checked they are making $47,337 a month on Patreon (more on that later).

Just realize that you are making yourself unavailable to MANY advertisers when your show goes hardcore R-rated.

If you don't list your show as explicit and Apple discovers it, you may be kicked out. If you list *one episode* as explicit, the *entire podcast* is considered explicit. According to Daniel J. Lewis of *The Audacity to Podcast* (theaudacitytopodcast.com), you are removed from Apple in the following countries for marking it explicit:

Bahrain	Nepal
Belarus	Oman
Brunei Darussalam	Qatar
Burkina Faso	Saudi Arabia
Chad	Tunisia
Egypt	United Arab Emirates
India	Uzbekistan
Jordan	Yemen
Lebanon	

While you may not think your target audience lives there, some of those countries have A LOT of people. I want you to go in with your eyes open.

NOBODY LIKES A BAD INFOMERCIAL

While I understand that you want to use your podcast to promote your product or service, the content can't be plug, plug, plug, and then plug. Nobody chooses to watch a bad infomercial if there are other options available.

Joe Vitale was a seasoned Internet marketer. He had a HUGE email list. When podcasting was taking off in early 2005, Joe decided to get in on the game. He created a twenty-minute podcast. I felt most of it involved heavy selling of his products. There was no useful information that I could use. There were no topics connected to my emotions and nothing that educated or entertained me. Joe sent it out to his giant email list and asked them to vote for him at Podcastalley.com, which was a directory of podcasts (this was before Apple Podcasts had come on to the scene). The site produced a Top 10 list, and Joe shot to number one immediately. Everyone asked, "Who is Joe Vitale?" People went to listen to his podcast. It was awful. Joe fell off the charts almost as quickly as he appeared. Remember, great content keeps people *coming back.*

In Cleveland (I live in Akron, Ohio), the top drive-time talk show host is Mike Trivisonno. There are few things that make me scratch my head like a promo for the Mike Trivisonno show ON HIS SHOW. Hello? I'm already listening; I'm here. My favorite was when I downloaded the "first hour" of his podcast; it was thirty-eight minutes. That's right—the other twenty-two minutes were commercials that (for reasons that confuse me) they cut out of the download. Twenty-two minutes is 37 percent of the broadcast. People still wonder why people are leaving radio for podcasts.

Comedian Conan O'Brien has a podcast called *Conan O'Brien Needs a Friend* (teamcoco.com/podcasts). He might think about renaming it *Conan O'Brien Needs Some Cash.* When I listened to an episode with fellow comedian Dana Carvey, the breakdown was as follows:

- 0–2:00 Advertisements
- 2:00–20:00 Interview with Dana
- 20:00–26:30 Advertisements
- 26:30–40:00 Interview with Dana
- 40:00–41:00 Credits for his staff
- 41:00–42:00 Promotions for other podcasts

This means ten and a half minutes of a forty-two-minute show was NOT Conan or Dana. Ten and a half minutes of ads calculate to 25 percent of the show. For me, I can tolerate the ads at the beginning. When he gets to the mid-roll ads about halfway through his *six-minute* segment of ads, I start questioning my choice of listening to his podcast. I know some people say they don't mind because he makes the ads entertaining, but for me, I can now say 25 percent of an episode being ads makes me start to twitch. If I hate the ads, I can sign up for Stitcher Premium for $4.99 a month (or $35.04 a year) and get the episodes ad-free (which could be the reason they have so many).

CONTENT THAT FORWARDS YOUR GOAL WHILE ENTICING YOUR AUDIENCE

The Trader Joe's grocery chain has a podcast called *Inside Trader Joe's* where (you guessed it) they share stories about what is happening at Trader Joe's. One episode shared how they are swapping out refrigeration units for ones that are better for the environment. Why? Because people who shop at Trader Joe's are into healthy eating and a healthy planet. When they hear that Trader Joe's is putting their money with their mouth is, they love the brand even more and tell their friends.

John Deere has a podcast, but you won't hear a giant commercial for tractors. Instead, you might hear them talk about the rising number of farmers committing suicide and how farmers can get help. They want farmers to be successful. Why? Because successful farmers buy more tractors.

Maytag (who makes washing machines) had a podcast at one point. Their podcast included topics that families (who typically have a lot of dirty clothes) would appreciate. Topics included how to get your children to brush their teeth longer, etc. Through their podcast, Maytag became trusted friends with great advice. When it comes time to buy a new washer, people will remember their trusted Maytag Company.

When you know the WHY of your podcast, and you understand what your audience wants to talk about, you can find those topics that engage your audience while helping you achieve your goal. Your audience might want to talk about recipes (but that doesn't forward you toward your goal). You might want to talk about email conversions and sales funnels for your business (but your audience doesn't care about that). What are the topics that your audience wants to hear that help position you in the right direction? Those are the items that you want to emphasize.

Another example of this would be the *Busy Mom Podcast* (I'm making this up) that is a daily show where the episodes last forty minutes. What busy mom has forty minutes a day to listen to a daily podcast? You want a win-win for both you and your audience.

THE LAW OF RECIPROCITY

Why do a podcast? It has to do with the Law of Reciprocity. Wikipedia defines *reciprocity* as "Responding to a positive action with another positive action and responding to a negative action with another negative one." Reciprocity is doing something nice for someone who has done something nice for you.

Bill Strand does the *Chameleon Breeder* podcast (chameleonbreeder.com). Bill creates cages and stands for chameleons. Bill told me that his audience sends messages such as "We could purchase these cages for less money from people overseas, but we want to support you and your show." Bill also told me he was going to slow down production on his show as his manufacturer couldn't keep up with the demand. I told him to get a new (or an additional) manufacturer.

MORE TOUCHES EQUALS MORE SALES

Doing three ten-minute shows spread across the week may lead to more sales than a thirty-minute show once a week. The more your audience consumes your brand, the more times you can remind them to make a purchase. By engaging your audience more frequently, it keeps your name in front of them, and this may lead to more sales. Keep in mind that with a shorter show, the promotional portion of your podcast needs to be shorter as well. I had an "outro" that I played at the end of my *Weekly Web Tools* podcasts. It mentioned how to contact me, and then I did a sixty-second spot on the "sponsor" (affiliate). I later cut the show length from fifteen minutes to five. Consequently, I had to redo the outro, as the previous outro could've been 25 percent of my total episode length (and who do I think I am, Conan O'Brien?).

FEED THE SEARCH ENGINES

It does take some time to record and publish a podcast. One of the things you can do to keep search engines coming back is to write a post that describes your episode (called "show notes"). Show notes give more things for visitors and, more importantly, search engines (Google, Bing) to find. Once visitors find you, hopefully, they will see the "Click to listen" button on your website that will entice them to stick around. Hopefully they will see the Apple/ Android Podcasts links on your website and subscribe. This is one of the reason podcasting can boost your SEO rankings. Google sees people coming to your site and staying longer. They conclude this must be great content. They don't know people are on the site longer because they are listening to your podcast.

According to WordPress SEO by Yoast (a copywriting plug-in for WordPress), when you post an episode, you should be typing around 300 words to describe it. More valuable words will serve as "food" for search engines. When I researched some of the top bloggers, their average word count was 700 words per post.

When it comes to your website, be it a new podcast or a blog post, you should be updating your website weekly at the minimum.

SUMMARY

- To grow your audience, identify your target listener, go to where they are, and LISTEN to what they are talking about. Identify what they would want in their podcast then give it to them. Go to where they are and make friends and bring value to the conversations. THEN tell them about your show.
- The way to stand out and get people talking about you is to deliver great content.
- While poor content delivered professionally may be temporarily tolerated, great content delivered in an unlistenable, unwatchable format will not.
- While you may be promoting a service or product, an episode that is more promotion than standard content will annoy your audience. Keep advertisements short and to the point.
- Adding show notes to your website provides "food" for search engines like Google and Bing.
- While you are free to be as explicit as you want, you might want to consider if the need to drop F-bombs in your show is worth the potential loss of audience and sponsorship opportunities.
- If your audio quality forces your audience to adjust whatever device they are using to listen, they won't stick around for long.
- People are in a hurry. Get to the point, and don't be boring.

How to Make Money with a Podcast

There are several ways to make money with your podcast once you've built up that audience. Here they are in order of impact:

1. Sell your own products
2. Live events
3. Sell other people's products (affiliates)
4. Sponsors
5. Donations and crowdfunding
6. Opportunities
7. Free stuff

Most people jump to sponsors first because we are conditioned to think like radio and radio has sponsors. If you want a "big" sponsor, then your episodes need to have at least 5,000 downloads after thirty days of being published. Currently, less than 10 percent of podcasts get those kinds of numbers. With that small of a percentage, for most podcasters, advertisers are not the top way to make money with your show.

Now let's dive into those deeper.

5

Selling Your Products

By consistently bringing value to your audience, they will know, like, and trust you. Consequently, when you develop a product of your own, they will be champing at the bit to purchase it.

You also can get direct feedback from your audience, ensuring that the product you create fits a need for them. *You no longer guess if this will sell.* Because you live, eat, and breathe in your niche, and know your audience at a whole new level, the item will sell.

Daniel J. Lewis of *The Audacity to Podcast* (theaudacitytopodcast.com) realized that his audience was very focused on their reviews in the Apple Podcasts app. He hired some developers to create what is now My Podcast Reviews (mypodcastreviews.com) and thought it would cost in the low four figures. In the end it cost him six times what he thought it was going to cost. However, Daniel KNEW that his audience wanted this tool, so he kept investing time and money into the system, which now has more than paid for itself and is a consistent part of his revenue stream. By knowing (not guessing) his audience would buy it, he could invest (almost) worry-free.

In his June 2019 income report, John Lee Dumas notes that his three books (*Freedom Journal, Mastery Journal, Podcast Journal*) sold 435 copies for a total of $11,747 for ONE MONTH. Why? These books were written based on feedback he received from his audience. According to an article in the *Huffington Post*[1], "The average US nonfiction book is now selling less than

---

1   BJ Gallagher, "The Ten Awful Truths—and the Ten Wonderful Truths—About Book Publishing," *HuffPost*, last updated December 6, 2017, https://www.huffpost.com/entry/book-publishing_b_1394159.

250 copies per year[2]," and this was echoed in an article from the Nonfiction Authors Association.

Cathy Heller is a singer who hosts the podcast *Don't Keep Your Day Job* (dontkeepyourdayjob.com), and when I interviewed her, she explained how hard it is to make a living as a musician. When she dove headfirst into the music business, she discovered that people were succeeding by licensing their music to TV and movies. She submitted her music successfully hundreds of times to have it used in films, TV, and ads. As she had discovered a solution for musicians, this led to her starting an agency to help get additional musicians' music placed (catchthemoonmusic.com). That lead to her hosting live events for musicians. None of this would've happened if she didn't understand what her audience wanted. First, she had to understand the type of music being used in TV and films (so understand what your target audience needs) and later she knew she could fill the need of struggling musicians. In both cases she is solving a problem.

In the same way that Netflix can create content that you like (because they know what you watch and enjoy), creating content in a vacuum where you hope your audience will love it is a thing of the past.

You will also find the pains of your audience through your relationship with them. I did audio editing in the early days of podcasting. Why? Because my audience said, "I just want to talk into the microphone, do you know someone who could do the rest?" and I did (me). I would not have known that without starting my podcast and getting to know my audience. They will tell you what they need, and you then give it to them.

My *School of Podcasting* show drives people to my membership site. As part of the membership site, I do live group coaching. In those coaching sessions, I see what my audience needs. I see where they get stuck. This wider view results in me creating tutorials to help solve their problems, and it helps me create better content for my podcast, which drives people to my membership site.

Does podcasting work? I offer a coupon code to my listeners in my podcast. I never put it in print. When people join the School of Podcasting, 70 percent of them use the coupon.

---

2   Stephanie Chandler, "How many books can you expect to sell? The truth about book sales and the keys to generating income from publishing," Nonfiction Authors Association, October 3, 2019, https://nonfictionauthorsassociation.com/how-many-books-can-you-expect-to-sell-the-truth-about-book-sales-and-the-keys-to-generating-income-from-publishing/.

Daniel J. Lewis of *The Audacity to Podcast* listened to his audience, and while they didn't want his web design services that I mentioned at the beginning of the book, he did notice a few things they needed. Consequently, he created the courses SEO for Podcasters, Zoom H6 for Podcasters, and My Podcast Reviews, as well as a WordPress plug-in called Social Subscribe and Follow. Daniel got into podcasting thinking it would boost his web design business (it didn't), but he discovered pains that his audience had and created products to solve them. He created a membership site called Podcasters' Society. Podcasters' Society is a niche membership site that is NOT about launching a podcast; it focuses on growing the show you've launched.

Take advantage of the resource that is your audience and do your research. The first product I ever launched was a "Digital Résumé." It was a self-running tutorial on a CD-ROM (this was a while ago). My family and friends told me I should sell them online. I did no research and built a website. Days later (after spending HOURS building the site, graphics, etc.) I did a quick Google search and found that not only was I late to the game, but other products were better and less expensive. Use your audience as a resource to create products they will buy (and don't trust your friends or parents).

Darren Dake started his podcast *Coroner Talk* (coronertalk.com) as a coroner in Missouri. He didn't have a huge social following. He was not a celebrity. His show is about death scene investigation (very niche). As you might imagine, coroners don't have many opportunities to talk about their job to other coroners. He started this show in 2014 (way before the true crime genre was the hot thing) and just wanted to talk death scene investigation and swap insights and strategies with other coroners. Darren's podcast resulted in him being asked to speak to more and more groups. In 2015 the exposure Darren got from his podcast (and speaking gigs where he was building relationships) lead to him taking the position as the Director of Training for the Association of Deputy Sheriffs for the state of Missouri. The deeper Darren got into his niche, the more he saw a need.

The training to become a coroner was limited. In some cases, you needed to be recertified on a yearly basis, but there was a lack of places and offerings to be recertified. If you wanted any kind of training to become a coroner and get into the field, there wasn't any. Darren (like Kathy Heller I mentioned above) didn't have a product when he started his podcast, but he saw a need and hole that needed to be filled.

Darren started the Death Investigation Academy (ditacademy.org) in a spare bedroom. Then as his training became more popular, he migrated his academy to a small office in his church. In 2018 Darren purchased a building to house the Academy. This building has classrooms, but it also has an audio and video production as he is offering training online. Fast-forward five years and Darren has quit his job (as he still travels and speaks to groups), and the Death Investigation Academy is now the mandated basic training for several states and districts across the country for coroners and medical examiner investigators.

When I was chatting with Darren he said, "In our surveys we always ask students how they heard about our Academy and we are getting a large number of employer friend referrals now (*relationships*), but we still get over half saying they first heard about it from our podcast. It's just so interesting that it all absolutely truthfully started from a podcast." I won't disclose how much money Darren is making, but if his checks were your checks, you'd have a very large smile on your face.

What I love about Darren's story is that he used what he had. He didn't wait until he could purchase a building to start his academy. He didn't spend thousands of dollars on equipment to make his podcast. You start where you are and upgrade as you go. You can hear an early interview I did with Darren in 2015 at schoolofpodcasting.com/444.

SELLING A BOOK

I've seen many podcasters take episodes and have them transcribed. They send the transcripts over to an editor and add some additional information, and you have an instant book. Howard Stern used this strategy for his latest book, *Howard Stern Returns*. While this is an "easy" book to write, I'm not sure it's WOW content.

Writing a book is a little bit like podcasting. You think writing the book is the hard part, when the truth is, getting people to buy it is the hard part. However, when you have your audience helping you along the way, it becomes easier. You can have them vote on different book covers. You might find out that there are people in your audience that might offer to do the editing, layout, and graphics for a discounted rate. Maybe some of your audience members would be interested in reading early drafts and providing feedback, making them into a sort of focus group dedicated to refining your manuscript.

The actual writing part is simple. You make a list of all the topics you want to cover. Then under each topic, you add any subtopics. Once that is complete, go back and expand each subtopic. When you're done, the writing part is over, and you are off to editing.

A great example of someone who is using a podcast to generate income is Dave "The Kindlepreneur" Chessen. His podcast, *The Book Marketing Show,* is all about book publishing (kindlepreneur.com/podcast/). He brings people on each episode to give real-life examples from the publishing world. He often will give tips and insights on his show that help demonstrate the power of his software and tools that he has for authors. You can find my interview with David at profitfromourpodcast.com/14.

Additional resources about book marketing include Daniel Hall's *Real Fast Results* podcast at realfastresults.com/ or Amy Collins's *Free Advice Friday* at https://newshelves.com/faf/.

SELLING CONSULTING

Selling consulting is an area that I do regularly, and you can boost your client list through podcasting. As a consultant you often answer the same question over and over. The good news is now you can take those questions and turn them into episodes. Turning frequently asked questions into episodes enables you to answer the question once, and if someone asks the question you can briefly answer it, and state, "for more information see this episode of our podcast" (with a link).

Now the potential client gets their answer, and probably a few other answers to questions they didn't know they had. They get to know you. You appear to know what you're talking about and seem very helpful.

You get to flex your knowledge in front of your target audience.

I once had someone call me (I have a phone number on my website) and after I said "Hello," the caller said, "I just drove from Minnesota to South Carolina listening to all of your episodes. I'm still working on my podcast idea, but I wanted to let you know YOU ARE MY GUY."

As I write this, I have thousands of episodes, if you count all my shows. If you look at the School of Podcasting, I just went over 700 episodes. When I look at my numbers for the month, close to 60 percent of my episodes are not from episodes released this month. My first episode from 2005, titled "Your First Podcast Typically Stinks," still gets downloaded fifteen years after its release.

You're not just recording audio. You are creating assets. Assets that work for you all over the world, twenty-four hours a day, seven days a week. In most cases your podcast is not your business, it's your *business card*.

You can say things like "If you need coaching, reach out to me at my website" (link). Some of your audience doesn't understand what "coaching" means. Natalie Eckdahl from the *Biz Chix* podcast (bizchix.com) has an easy way to help her audience understand what kind of coaching she does. She records them and publishes them as episodes. Here again, you get to strut how much knowledge you have and help your client. Your audience may think, *Wow, I had that same problem—awesome! I wonder if she could help me with this issue* . . . And they reach out.

SELLING A SERVICE

Can you listen to my podcast and tell me if it's good? I got that question via email. Then I got another one and another. Some people would hire me to listen to their show and then do a consulting call to get the results. The bottom line is I saw a service that people wanted.

I reached out to a friend of mine, Erik K. Johnson, who has thirty years' experience in radio and hosts the *Podcast Talent Coach* show (podcasttalentcoach.com). Erik joined me on the *Podcast Review Show* (podcastreviewshow.com) where (for a discounted price) you get TWO consultants to go over your podcast and website from head to toe. Why the discount? Because we taped these sessions and put them out publicly. These live consulting calls not only helped the guest, but it gave them exposure. It allowed us to show off our expertise, and in some cases, this led to more private consulting and more people signing up for the School of Podcasting.

Then I had a few people who couldn't afford it. As a joke, I started the *Podcast Rodeo Show* where I listen to the first few minutes of your podcast and see if I can hang on. The price? Five dollars. There is no show prep. The show is recorded live. What you are hearing are honest first impressions. At the end of the show, I point out that if you want a FULL review, check out the *Podcast Review Show*. I have seen people go up the funnel from the *Podcast Rodeo Show* to the *Podcast Review Show* and then on to more consulting. The *Podcast Rodeo Show* got people talking about it as I give HONEST reviews (not like Mom).

Here again, if I hadn't started and jumped in, I wouldn't have known there was a need for this service. Because I had gained the audience's loyalty and trust, they use the service.

You might be thinking, *But how do you sell without creating an infomercial?* You have to let people know what you do. You can't expect to get speaking gigs if you don't mention that you are available for them. You won't get any coaching clients if you don't mention you are a coach. There are subtle ways of doing this without being an infomercial or screaming THIS SUNDAY! SUNDAY! SUNDAY! If you can explain a point you are making with a story, DO IT. Simply saying, "I was working with a client the other day, and they had this issue . . ." BOOM—your audience now knows you are available for consulting. Another example, "I was speaking to a group of high school kids in Ohio, and one of them asked me . . ." BOOM—your audience now knows you are available for speaking engagements.

If you're thinking, *Well, I put a link to the webinar on the website,* you need to realize that there are people who find your show via a Google search and subscribe to your show—without ever visiting your website.

SELLING A PRODUCT YOU MANUFACTURE

The big lesson you need to learn here is remember podcasting has a *global* audience. George Hrab is a musician who does a science-based comedy show called the *Geologic Podcast* (georgehrab.com). George had a new CD release and explained on his podcast (where he occasionally performs original music) that one of the CDs had a golden ticket (tipping his hat to Willy Wonka) and whoever got the golden ticket would have George perform in their living room (or venue of choice). George lives in Bethlehem, Pennsylvania, and where did the lucky listener who got the golden ticket live? Helsinki, Finland.

What did George do? He announced he was coming and worked with his audience to set up a five-city "Golden Ticket" tour to help pay the cost.

SELLING SWAG

Swag is stuff with your logo on it. T-shirts, mugs, mousepads, coasters, stickers, etc. can all be considered swag. In talking with podcasters for over a decade I only know of one person who was able to sell more than a handful. That is Gordon Rochford of *Those Conspiracy Guys* podcast (thoseconspiracyguys.com). Gordon may have an episode with a bit of an inside joke or catchphrase. For example, one thing you might hear on the show is "That sh*t is bananas."

Consequently, they have a T-shirt with a banana peel filled with poo. If you are a fan of the show and you see another person wearing that shirt, you have an instant bond as you both can identify each other as fans of the show. Gordon has used Fiverr (fiverr.com) to hire artists to create designs that they turn in to shirts using Tee Public (podclick.me/teepublic). Selling T-shirts is one of those things where you might have one shirt that hits home and some that get zero sales.

One of my favorite examples of a T-shirt is from the *Latter-Day Lesbian* podcast (latterdaylesbian.org). They received a one-star review in Apple Podcasts. The review stated, "Doing the work of the Adversary." What did they do? They put the name of the podcast under the review and turned it into a T-shirt. They took what was a negative comment and turned it into a battle cry that their fans can proudly wear.

Mark Des Cotes of podcastbranding.co has created shirts for his show, and podcast-related shirts, and his results were "meh." Mark is a great designer (the shirts look amazing), and if he can't move shirts, nobody can. I say this to help you set expectations when you launch your shirt. You can often sell more if they are a limited edition. The good news is you can create a design and upload it to your store, and that's the only effort needed.

Don't overlook your fan base. There are people in your audience that want to help you succeed. Adam Curry and John C. Dvorak get jingles for segments all the time sent in from their audience. Their audience also generates artwork for the show. When your audience is involved with the creation of the swag, they are more likely to buy it and promote it.

SELLING A MEMBERSHIP SITE

We need to clarify here the difference between selling a course and selling a membership site. With a membership site, you create content on an ongoing basis, and your members pay a recurring fee (typically monthly or yearly) to access the content. Unlike an online course, there is no ending point for a membership site, and you are expected to continue to add new content to your membership site indefinitely.

Membership sites can be a nice stream of income. It sounds like it is passive, and it can be. If I have a course that teaches people about podcast equipment, they can take the course, buy their equipment, and their problem is solved. With my School of Podcasting website, I do both. I sell courses that solve problems that you can buy individually, or you can buy a membership package that includes ALL my courses, live group coaching, and a private Facebook group.

Many people think they want to launch a membership site when what they want is a community. A community site is not a one and done. My

School of Podcasting site is a *community*. Yes, there are more than a dozen video courses there that you can go through, but you also get access to a private Facebook group where you can network with people, and you get access to group coaching with me. If you want people to stick around, you need to build a community. Having a community can be HUGE for people who are solopreneurs and possibly work from home and have almost zero interaction with people. It's a way to meet and interact with people without getting out and meeting and interacting with people.

Group coaching is something I enjoy. While you are the "expert" (as it is your membership site), you often are just the facilitator of the conversations and other members of the community can chime in on answers.

For example, if someone wants me to answer a question on Photoshop, I can answer a few very basic questions, but I don't use it enough to do any advanced functions. This is where a member of my community can be on the webinar, share their screen, and answer the more advanced questions.

In the private Facebook group, I share posts of what is happening in the podcast industry so people can stay up to date. People will make polls so the community can vote on their favorite artwork for their podcast. The title of this book was shaped using feedback from members of my Facebook group. I often will make a rough draft of a video and get feedback before adding the "official" video to a course.

I also provide a venue for people to share their podcast and get feedback. The feedback happens in a controlled fashion, so it's not a giant wall of self-promotion.

By having live coaching, a Facebook group, and constructive feedback services, it entices people to stay long after they have gone through all the courses.

INSIGHTS FROM RUNNING MEMBERSHIP SITES

When I first launched the School of Podcasting, I tried many different plugins for WordPress and landed on Digital Access Pass. The tool is super flexible, and I'll talk more about it in the chapter on tools. I wanted to share some insights into running a website.

I recommend having a separate website for your membership site. I used to have all the tutorials on the School of Podcasting website. When I looked at the back end, I had to keep track of which content was private and which was public. If you have different packages, you have to keep track of everything. It can become quite a headache.

You've probably heard the old KISS approach (Keep it Simple, Stupid). There is a reason that the old saying is still around. It makes a lot of sense.

I was trying an experiment for a weight loss show I do call *Logical Weight Loss*. I was adding a community, and what I did to solve the confusion of which posts were or were not private was to create a second membership site for the show. By having the membership site separate from the original website, it made life SO MUCH EASIER. When I logged into the membership site, EVERYTHING in it was private. I also didn't have to work with any conflicts with plug-ins, and life was just easier.

One day I went to log into my School of Podcasting WordPress site, and couldn't. It was giving me an error message. It was just S-L-O-W. Something was very wrong. In the end, it turned out that some malicious site was trying to hack me. I mentioned at the beginning of the book that I have a love/hate relationship with WordPress. I love that it is super flexible, and its popularity inspires people to make tools, themes, and plug-ins that work with WordPress. It is this popularity that also puts a bull's-eye on its back.

Anything that involves making me money, I moved off my WordPress site. That is just my opinion. I work with many podcasters who use WordPress, and I don't see many—but I do see some—websites that have the "white screen of death," where WordPress has a bad day. I see plug-ins that cause weird issues. Again, there are not a lot of these, but I don't want to take the chance that my business gets temporarily ruined by a plug-in. I'll talk more about this in the tools section, as one tool you NEED is a backup tool that makes backing up the site easy and effectively.

You want to make it super easy to get going with your membership site. Bringing on new members is often referred to as the "onboarding" process. You should create a page of frequently asked questions (one of which should be how to leave your membership site). As you get more questions, add them to the list (or make your site easier, so these questions don't get asked).

I know you just read a paragraph that said to make it easy to leave your site, and you might be thinking, *WHAT?!* You want customers who WANT to be in your community because they love the value. You don't want them there because they can't find the door to leave. You don't want your membership site to be like an escape room where people panic trying to leave before their membership is charged again.

Speaking of avoiding certain complaints, if you have an option for people to sign up for a membership that renews once a year, you want to set up some automation to remind them before it renews that it's going to renew (and how to unsubscribe). Why? A monthly fee may trigger your member to say, "Oh, I need to take care of that later" (and they may forget about it). A person charged for a year will have an "I need to take care of this NOW" reaction (and will). If you want to avoid the "Hey, my card just got charged" email from your yearly subscriber, then you should notify them before it renews. You could set up an email list for subscribers that sends a reminder email for those who signed up for a year (monthly members don't need a reminder as they get one on their credit card each month).

A membership tool will allow you to create an email that your members receive when they sign up. Take advantage of that and give super clear directions on how to get started. Have a link to a video that explains how to get started. You want it to be super clear, super easy.

While I will talk more about tools for membership sites, one I love (and it's free) is Freshdesk, which is a ticketing/frequently asked question tool (freshdesk.com). There is an app, and you can set notifications so that if someone creates a ticket, you get notified. This also helps you avoid clogging your email inbox (although you can receive notifications via email).

If you are looking to take a deep dive into membership sites, check out Mike Morrison and Callie Willows of the Membership Academy. Mike and his partner have a ton of information on running a successful membership site based on years of experience. See membershipacademy.com.

As I said before, more about membership sites in the appendix.

CHARGING YOUR GUESTS TO APPEAR ON YOUR SHOW

Just thinking about this strategy makes me throw up in my mouth (just a little bit). Charging guests to appear on your show is somewhat new. I believe the motivation for this is ego. When you compare your show to others, it rarely if ever results in something positive. Comparison is the number one killer of podcast attitudes. For whatever reason, someone compared themselves to another successful show, and now they feel their show *deserves* to earn income because another show is earning income. This can really hurt if you've been podcasting longer than the other show. I have been playing the guitar longer then Justin Bieber. Does that mean I should earn more than him? Oh wait, he has the talent and a super engaged audience.

Why do people feel this is an honest strategy? Because you are giving them exposure (among other reasons I'll get into). I guess they don't feel that the guest giving value in exchange for some exposure is a fair trade. I know of a few people who are doing this, and I couldn't disagree more. I wasn't going to include this idea in the book, but I know you may hear about it and I wanted to explain why I feel it's a bad idea. Here is why:

1. If you are hurting for cash, you are likely to have people on your show that do not provide value for your audience.
2. You need to specify for Federal Trade Commission (FTC) purposes that you are being paid to have this person on your show, in the same way that celebrities must let people know they are getting paid for holding a product on Instagram. This appearance will be somewhat like the beginning of an infomercial (because that's what it is): "The following conversation was paid for by (guest's name)."

Why Are People Advocating This Idea?

Too many requests. If you're getting a ton of requests to be on your show, I understand adding an "appearance fee" will weed out the bad apples. You can set up a form on your show site (see forms.google.com) and create an in-depth questionnaire that will weed out people who don't fit your audience for free.

Because it takes time away from their family. If you are taking time away from your family to prepare and record (to the point it is causes stress), quit podcasting (immediately) as you don't have enough time. #familyfirst

A growing audience that spans thousands of downloads per month. When I see this reason, a red flag goes up. As I mentioned earlier, 60 percent of my downloads come from episodes not released in the current month. When people quote monthly numbers, they are either uninformed on how to track progress (episode totals, not monthly totals) or their ego loves the monthly totals because they are bigger.

No one is going to hire me to consult for their business based on being a fun host on an engaging show. If you're not getting the results you want, it means your content is not in alignment with your goal of being a business consultant. If you want to be a business consultant, do a solo show and answer common questions you run across as a business consultant. Have one of your clients do a live coaching call for a discounted rate. Interviewing other business owners does not paint you as an expert. It paints *them* as an expert.

Earlier I mentioned Natalie Eckdahl (bizchix.com), who provides discounted coaching. Her guests are paying to be on the show. What's the difference? Natalie is providing value to the guest in the form of coaching. I just feel that is different from interviewing someone. I also feel there is more value in listening to a coaching call. My biggest fear with "pay to be a guest" is you're going to interview someone who doesn't deliver value to your audience. Natalie is interviewing her target audience, so I know her target audience is getting value from the call (because they are just like the guest). The biggest difference is one is a coaching call (which you are expected to pay for), and the other is an interview (which is typically free).

Hosting costs: The hosting costs for both the website and keeping the podcast online for the world to download. A website is around $20/month, a media host is around $20/month, and a domain is around $20/year. You spend more money going golfing on the weekend.

Every podcaster starts with zero downloads and integrity. If I hear a guest on your show who does not deliver value, and I know you got paid?

That is my definition of selling out.

It's your brand. It's your reputation. Do with it what you want.

Trust is the basis of relationships. I once was the stepfather of a child who lied to me and my then-wife. It took quite a while before we didn't second-guess everything coming out of his mouth. Do you want to throw your integrity away for money that will be used with your next house payment (or next tank of gas)? Companies spend ten times the budget to get back a customer than to keep them in the first place.

This is worth repeating. The worst thing you can do for your podcast is to compare it to someone else.

Don't focus on another podcast.

Focus on your audience.

PRICING YOUR PRODUCTS AND SERVICES

When I first launched the School of Podcasting, it was five dollars a month. I believed that if I could get a hundred people to sign up, it would be five hundred dollars a month. I was in college at the time, and that would pay for food, gas, books, etc.

I opened the doors, and nobody came in. How could this be? I was the *only person teaching people how to podcast in 2005.*

I had two problems. The first was the timing. I had to do a HUGE amount of education to get people to understand what a podcast was (let alone if they wanted to start one).

The second one was my pricing. A friend of mine asked me a very good question. "What can you buy online for five dollars?" I thought about it. There wasn't much (of value). While I had the heart of a teacher (still do), when my visitors came to my website, they could've easily thought, *This must not be any good because it's only five dollars.* Pricing can establish value in the mind of the customer. I'm not going to pay twenty dollars for a four-pack of toilet paper. Why? Because I can easily look at the other options on the shelves and judge quality. If there is nothing else to compare you to and your price is super low, people may very well use the price as a stand-in for quality.

I raised my price to twenty dollars per month. I got more business. However, I found that some of my members were taking their sweet time creating their podcasts. My goal is that the members of the School of Podcasting will help promote the website. If they don't end up creating an actual podcast, they don't generate any buzz, and nobody asks them, "How did you learn to podcast?"

I raised my price to forty-nine dollars per month and got more members than I did at a lower price. These members were also more inspired and focused and "hungry" to get started.

The book *Paying to Win,* by CEO A. G. Laley and Roger Martin, explains how Proctor and Gamble relaunched the Olay brand. They tested three prices.

- At $12.99, it was affordable to the average user and the sales were okay.
- At $15.99, they had priced themselves out of the average user, and they weren't expensive enough to attract the attention of the prestige shopper.
- They changed the price to $18.99. This price was a good value for a *premium product.* It was also slightly affordable for the mass market. The brand went on to be a business worth $2.4 billion.

How Do You Know If You're Not Charging Enough?

Go back to how you picked your price. If you picked your number because the rent is due, and you need money NOW, you probably picked the wrong price.

If you quote someone a price and they don't blink, you probably could have said a higher number. Keep raising your price until someone says no. That's a pretty good barometer. Many people don't like this, as it means they miss out on business (at least once). They are not thinking long-term. Yes, you lost a potential client, but the increase in pricing will pay for itself over time.

The other way to know you're not charging enough is if you hear "You need to raise your prices" from a customer more than once. You should believe them. That's what I heard about the *Podcast Review Show* service (podcastreviewshow.com).

As someone with a teaching background, my DNA is focused on helping people. Money is nice, but I feel great when I help someone learn something new, that enables them to do more. I fell victim to my "helper's gene" when I priced the *Podcast Review Show*. As I previously mentioned, I do this with a cohost (Erik K. Johnson from podcasttalentcoach.com). You are getting TWO consultants for the price of a HALF. I'm doubling the price and it hasn't hurt our business. Why did we price it so low? The goal is to introduce people to coaching and get them into our sales funnel. We've had a few people say, "You need to raise your price," and we are.

Famed sales trainer Brian Tracy (briantracy.com) says, "Do market research on your competitors to determine the right price. If you have a high-priced product, be prepared to over-deliver quality to your customers. Price can be determined by 'perceived value' of your product. If you can make your product seem superior to your competitors, you can charge a higher price."

Let Your Audience Set the Price

Greg Fitzsimmons is a well-established comedian, author, and podcaster. When he first started his podcast, he made a joke that if someone sent him ten dollars, they could sponsor a spot on his show. Someone did, and he did. The next time he decided to take his spot to eBay. This time instead of ten dollars, he received $212 as the final bid amount. The description of what you receive is:

> *You've heard of the Fitzdog Radio Podcast; now you can be ON the Fitzdog Radio Podcast!*
>
> *Receive a short mention on FitzDog Radio Podcast. You can promote a product or send a greeting to a friend or loved one.*

> *All you have to do is join the bidding war and put up your highest bid on this prime audio real estate. The winner will be notified and then must come up with a short plug, being a sentence or two. Once you have provided your special plug, it will be recorded by comedian Greg Fitzsimmons and aired on the next Fitzdog Radio Podcast.*

The beginning bid started at 99 cents, and thirty-two bids later, Greg closed his auction at $212. If you're not sure what to charge, maybe you should let your audience decide the value.

SUMMARY

- Selling your own products is the best way to make money with your podcast. You leverage the trust you have built with your audience and are selling items with no go-between. You are selling direct to consumer. You do have to let people know you have products and services available. Starting a podcast is not a "build it, and they will come" type of situation. You need to remember you are talking to a global audience and factor in shipping costs if you agree to ship overseas.

- You need to do some research to see what your competition is and how much they charge. While you may be tempted to cut your prices to stand out, do you want to be known as the "Walmart" of your niche?

6

Sponsorship

Many people jump to sponsorship when it comes to podcasting. Host-read ads can be very lucrative, depending on the size of the audience and how niche the topic is.

THE POWER OF THE NICHE

The more niche you are, the more you can charge. Therefore, it's so important to understand your audience and what they want. When an advertiser approaches, you can say with confidence, "That is the type of person who listens to my show," and you can charge a premium.

Right Product—Right Audience

Glenn Hebert of the Horse Radio Network explains how one of his manufacturers was advertising in magazines and not selling any of his products (manure forks). Glenn's audience was using this type of product when they listened to his show. Glenn explained how this product (shakenfork.com) is motorized and self-cleaning, and the product flew off the shelves. The sponsors purchased a year in advance, and now not ONLY advertises with Glenn but cohosts the *Horse Husband* show with Glenn once a month. When he is cohosting he sells more product on those days than any other day of the month. It's the right product for the right audience.

The Target Audience in the Palm of Your Hand

Mark Bologna hosts the *Beyond Bourbon Street* podcast (beyondbourbonst. com), where he explores the food, music, places, people, and events that make New Orleans unique. Mark has local companies wanting to sponsor his show (as it's all about their city). Mark will make a mid-five-figure income from advertising on his podcast, and he only does two episodes per month. How? The power of the niche. Mark, *without a doubt,* has their target audience.

DOES PODCAST ADVERTISING WORK?

Christine Miller of Two Chicks Walking (twochickswalkingtours.com) has told Mark that his show is the single biggest factor in her business *tripling in two years.* The first year, Mark didn't even charge them. He just sent his listeners to Two Chicks Walking because he knew his audience, and he knew they were a good fit.

Christine reached out to thank Mark, and that turned into a discussion of sponsoring the show that is a win-win for everyone.

When you have the right product for the right audience, the payoffs are huge for everyone involved.

THE INFLUENCE OF RADIO ADS ON PODCAST ADVERTISING

I stated earlier that less than 10 percent of podcasters get enough downloads per episode to warrant a sponsor. I need to clarify that statement. That is, if you are looking for "big" companies like Progressive Insurance, Harry's Razors, Zip Recruiter, Squarespace, or any of the other companies that you've probably heard ad nauseam. Many of those companies are looking for a minimum of 5,000 downloads per episode after thirty days of being published. Before we get into how to find sponsors, we need to understand how radio has influenced selling ads in podcasts. Hang on to your hats. We're going to do some math.

Cost per Thousand Downloads (CPM)

In radio, you paid a price for every one thousand listeners. This price is measured in CPM (cost per thousand, where the M stands for *mille*—a French word for "thousands"). In radio, if you had a CPM of $15 and your station had 10,000 listeners, the price of an ad was 10 × $15, or $150 per advertisement (numbers used are selected for easy math, not necessarily realistic rates).

Different Ad Positions and Titles

There are three primary advertisement locations:

Pre-Roll: This is an ad that runs at the very start of a show, typically just before or just after the episode's intro. It's a shorter read (twenty to thirty seconds), but most listeners will hear it because they're disinclined to skip forward, for fear of missing content. This spot typically has a lower rate than mid-roll ads.

Mid-Roll: This is an ad that runs in the middle of the program, once the primary content has started. These ads run longer than pre- and post-rolls (a minimum of sixty seconds), and hosts are more likely to integrate them directly into the flow of the show, injecting them with a little more creativity and spark. Consequently, this is the highest-priced spot position.

Post-Roll: This is an ad that runs at the end of the show, usually between the last content segment and any closing material. Post-rolls are typically shorter than mid-rolls and usually cost a bit less than pre-rolls. They are often purchased in combination with a pre-roll or post-roll spot in the same show to help reinforce a message introduced earlier in the episode, like an offer code or vanity URL. Post-rolls are typically the least expensive ad position. The ad reinforces the previous ads.

PODCAST DOWNLOAD NUMBERS

Do Downloads Equal Listeners?

Before we go talking about averages and such, let's address what counts as a download. When someone on a computer, website, phone, or tablet presses play (download) on the device, it counts as a download. If an app automatically downloads an episode, it counts as a download. There are a few exceptions that don't count.

Does this mean that a download equals a listener? No, but keep this in mind: Apple Podcasts (which has around 60 percent of the market) stops downloading episodes if you haven't consumed any of the previous five episodes. Does a newspaper do this? No. Does radio do this? No. Do magazines do this? No. You have no idea that someone has seen your ad in print or heard your ad on the radio, so people who bring up the "downloads don't equal listeners" are typically advertisers looking to get a better deal. Don't fall for it. If you don't want a podcast, you can unsubscribe at any time. There is no spam in podcasting. Edison Research presented information at Podcast Movement 2019 in Orlando that showed that listeners new to podcasting don't download the files or subscribe; instead they listen on the fly.

I am a podcast power listener. I subscribe to a TON of podcasts. As I look at my Overcast app on my iPhone, I see I have 330 episodes waiting for me to listen (and I will eventually listen to them all). Time-shifted listening is one of the most powerful aspects of podcasting, as it is a time-shifted medium. The content you created months ago, I can find and consume today. Remind potential sponsors of this when in negotiations.

What Are Good Download Numbers?

There is no "one size fits all" scale. A podcast about weight loss that gets 1,000 downloads might be considered a failure (as there is a HUGE audience for that topic). Take those 1,000 downloads and apply them to a podcast on pygmy ponies (a hyper-niche topic), and that's an amazing number.

As I write this in 2020, per Libsyn.com, the average is around 1,500 downloads after thirty days of being published. The median (meaning 50 percent get more and 50 percent get less) is around 150. This lower number is due to tons of people starting new podcasts and bringing the number down. At the beginning of the year, the numbers decline (as many new podcasts launch in January), and by December the number has risen (as podcast listening is somewhat of a winter sport, and the podcasts that launched in January are starting to grow their audience).

Now let's put the radio numbers into podcasting. Let's use a typical weekly podcaster who does four episodes a month. We will say they are getting 200 downloads per episode. They decide to run one advertisement per episode. Here's the math:

- At 200 downloads per weekly show, that is 800 downloads per month.
- $15 (the CPM rate from above) divided by 1,000 is $0.015 per download.
- 800 monthly downloads multiplied by $0.015 per download equals $12 per month.

This means you're eating mac and cheese again. Does this mean you should give up on advertisers? Absolutely not.

SETTING ADVERTISER EXPECTATIONS

In an episode titled "Exiled from the Industry He Helped Create" from the *Without Fail* podcast (from Gimlet Media: gimletmedia.com), Alex Blumberg interviews Jeff Ulrich, the founder of the Earwolf Network and Midroll (a company that was sold for $50 million). Jeff provides the story of their first advertising campaign with LegalZoom.

Jeff explained, "LegalZoom signed on to a three-month deal. And it was bad. I mean, that first month I thought they were going to ask for the money back. I was really upset and concerned. Nobody was putting in the offer code. So, LegalZoom canceled, they were like, 'It's not working. Sorry, we can't come back.' And then, three months after it ended, they called me up, and said, 'You're not going to believe this, but we have more conversions on the code in the three months after the ads ran than we did during the three months that the ads ran.'"

Why did it take so long for the ad campaign kick into gear? Alex Blumberg thinks the reasons might be:

- People listened to the episode on demand and weren't necessarily downloading the episodes and hearing those ads the minute the podcasts posted.
- People don't act on ads the first time they hear them. It takes repetition. A person has to hear an ad close to a dozen times before they act.
- The hosts gradually got better at reading the ads, which made the ads more convincing. These were the kind of lessons Jeff was learning over time. He would apply it back to the business to help it grow (and grow it did).

An advertiser who wants to run one spot for a single episode doesn't understand advertising. An advertiser looking to see action the minute the episode is released may be disappointed, and the host of the show should take some time getting comfortable with the ad copy and, if permitted by the advertiser (and if the advertiser is smart they will), be able to explain the product selling points in their own words.

When the podcast *Pod Save America* was on tour (more on that in a later chapter), the audience had paid to see them record an episode live. They had not planned on doing any advertisements (as they had paid to see the show). The crowd started calling out for ads, "Do Blue Apron! Let's hear Casper Mattress!" because the hosts had found a way to do ads that were entertaining while getting the selling points across.

SETTING PODCASTER EXPECTATIONS

As I write this, most sponsors are not approaching podcasts. The podcasts are chasing the sponsors. In some cases, you can work with an agency that will chase the sponsors for you.

REPORTING AND BILLING

I've had some advertisers on my *School of Podcasting* show. I know the feeling. You are ready to get paid. You recorded the spots in your episodes, and your work is done. Not so fast. Many advertisers want to hear the spots before writing you a check. I have an iPhone, and I love the app Overcast. I can listen to my podcast and copy a link that includes the time stamp. In other words, I can copy a link that will start the episodes where the ad starts.

GETTING PAID

You also want to establish terms with your advertiser. The podcast advertising network AdvertiseCast (advertisecast.com) pays podcasters thirty days after the ad has run on your show. This means you won't be getting paid for those ads in February until March (which probably means April), so plan accordingly. Some are even longer. According to Voxnest.com's FAQ, "You will receive each payment within 50 days after the end of the calendar month when the earned balance in your account equals or exceeds the applicable payment threshold. For example, if you start in January, you can expect your first payment mid to late March. You can then expect payments approximately every 30 days after that first payment."

In some cases, you may need to reach out and nudge your sponsor to send the check.

According to the Midroll website (midroll.com), CPM pricing ranges from eighteen to fifty dollars for an advertisement read by the host (creatively called "host read" ads). For our example, let's shoot right down the middle and use $35 CPM, or .035 per download

MORE FUN WITH MATH

The person who had 800 downloads per month now makes: 800 multiplied by .035 equals $28 per month. It's very hard to feed yourself (let alone a family) on $280 per month. The person with 8,000 downloads per month is taking home $280 per month. This demonstrates something that everyone now should see very clearly: CPM MAY WORK FOR RADIO, BUT IT DOES NOT WORK FOR 90 PERCENT OF PODCASTERS.

Also keep in mind, when you have an advertiser, you typically have to fill out a report for them stating how many downloads the episode(s) received, and a time stamp of when they can fast forward to hear the ad or a separate file of just the ad for them to consume. In other words, advertisers are more work for you. It's another detail that you need to keep track of if you want to be paid.

But wait: It gets *worse*.

DYNAMIC ADS

Dynamic ads are where you record an advertisement, go to your file, and select a place where your media host will insert the advertisement into your file. This ad can be for a certain time and be geo-targeted. If I'm a comedian, I can put an advertisement for my appearance at the Chuckle Hut in Clearwater, Florida, and have it appear for a month before my appearance and only put the ad in front of people in the Florida area. Then after that appearance, I can go back and insert a more generic advertisement. The technology is very powerful and very cool. Consequently, you do not get this in your typical media hosting package (but many media hosts have this option if you ask about the "Enterprise Version").

There is a slight problem with the phrase *dynamic ads*. It has a "guilty by association" reputation. The technology is cool, but the way it's used is not great, and neither are the payouts.

As many "generic" companies (mattresses, insurance, etc.) are using this technology, the "power of the niche" is gone. They are not looking for a specific audience, and consequently are not paying much to get in front of your audience. They also never get the volume level correct, which means you either blast the ears of your listeners or force them to turn up the volume. The problem with turning up the volume to hear the "too quiet" advertisement is when your show comes back on, you're going to blow their eardrums out.

I have an old show that I used to test a dynamic ad platform. First, you see that you will be paid fifty days after the month end. As I look at my dashboard in May, I note the last month for which I was paid was February. I had 200 episodes with a pre- and post-roll. I had 7,000 impressions. My CPM ranged from 1.37 to 4.26. I earned $11.07 on 7,000 downloads. That is $1.58 per thousand downloads (.00158 per download).

Now put that into the average podcaster who is getting 8,000 downloads per month. They take home $12.64 FOR THE MONTH.

When a company tries to get your attention with the promise of advertising, you might want to ask if they are using CPM, and if so, what is the average? If a company states, "We can have you making money from day one," this is the BS they are talking about.

Then ask yourself, is it worth potentially losing part of your audience because you are putting ads in front of them that are not targeted to them (because people in Europe love ads for stamps.com) for $2.75 an episode?

Before we move off this topic, let's not forget one thing that DOES make dynamics seem *slightly* more attractive. In some cases, you can get free media hosting in addition to getting paid by dynamic ads. If you were previously on a platform where you paid fifteen dollars a month and then made an additional eleven dollars, that is twenty-six dollars in your pocket. The idea is that you get free media hosting, and the ads will pay for the hosting and you get a little extra.

There is a word that people use to describe free media hosting companies that use this "business model": CLOSED.

Here is a list of free media hosting companies that have used this model:

- Podshow/Mevio 8/2005–4/2014 (116 months: $38.8 million spent)
- Podango 9/2006–12/2008 (27 months)
- Wildvoice.com 7/2006–7/2009 (36 months)
- Mypodcasts.com 2007–2011 (estimated 48 months)
- Audiometric.io 11/2012–8/2014 (21 months before being purchased by Panoply and taken off the market)
- Opinion Podcasting 11/2015–10/2017 (23 months)
- Zcat 1/2016–1/2019 (36 months)

That is an average of forty-three months. It's even less if we were to remove Mevio, which went through $38.8 million.

Anchor was funded in 2015 and purchased by Spotify in 2019 (42 months) for a reported $150 million.

Looking at the history of "Free Media Hosting," I would steer away from it. Free is just not a good business model.

MAKING A LIVING WITH ADVERTISEMENTS ALONE

People that are making a living from their podcast using JUST ads have common characteristics:

- They have been podcasting for years (3+).
- They produce many episodes per week (3–5).
- They have multiple ads per episode.
- They are in the top percentage of podcasters (hundreds of thousands of downloads per episode).
- They often have a team.
- Their shows are excellent (so people will tolerate the ads).
- They come with a prebuilt audience (celebrities).

CRITERIA FOR CHOOSING SPONSORS

Jeff Sanders (www.jeffsanders.com) is a podcaster, author, and speaker. He has been producing/hosting the *5 AM Miracle* podcast since 2015. Here are his thoughts on choosing sponsors:

Jeff Sanders:
Sponsors enable me to continue podcasting every week, and I love partnering with great brands.

1. Compatibility: My name, face, voice, and brand are all permanently attached to the companies I promote on my show. So, I only allow companies to sponsor my podcast who I believe offer products or services that fit my audience. If it's not a good fit for my people and my brand, I turn them down.

2. Legitimacy: I require every sponsor to provide me with access to their product so I can validate that what I promote is legitimate. I never accept money from companies without first ensuring that they are who they say they are and that their product or service is as good as I say it is on the show.

3. Quality: I have a high bar for quality, and most companies who want to market to my audience are not good enough. In effect, I end up turning down potential sponsors nearly every week.

4. Plant-Based: Yes, I am a vegan, and that aspect of my life matters a great deal to me. In effect, I do my best to work with companies who either (1) only offer products and services that are ethically viable for vegans (e.g., they do not use any animal products in their goods) OR (2) they offer a vegan option (e.g., Blue Apron's vegan meal plan). I turn down meat-based companies more often than any other potential sponsor.

5. Variety: I do my best to mix up the types of companies I work with to appeal to a broader audience base, and most companies prefer to be the only brand in the industry that I promote at any given time. My show is eclectic and diverse, and I prefer my sponsors to mimic that as well.

6. Content-First: My sponsor spots are placed in the middle of the episode so that the listener can get the value as quickly as possible. I do not allow pre-roll ads (before the episode) or post-roll ads (after the episode). Yes, I have done these in the past, but I quickly learned they were just too annoying. And yes, I do insert some promotional affiliate spots as pre-rolls on occasion, but those are my products or affiliates—not paid ads.

7. Host-Read: I read all of my own ads. I never accept pre-recorded ads from other voice actors. Reading all of my ads keeps the show authentic and keeps me connected to the brands I promote.

Other thoughts on sponsors.

Ad Agency: I have been working with AdvertiseCast exclusively since January 2019, and they have proven to be a great partner to help me find amazing companies to sponsor the show. I have sold my own ads in the past, and I still do on occasion, but it's a marvelous thing to partner with great people who understand your values and goals.

Ad-Free: I do offer an ad-free version of my podcast on Patreon, though not a single listener has taken me up on the offer. I'm still fascinated by the fact that 99 percent of all podcast listeners worldwide prefer podcasts with ads over paid subscriptions without ads. Some podcasts defy this norm, but most do not.

Feedback: I always accept feedback on my sponsors, and it's great to hear when listeners have found the ads valuable because they really do get a great deal from a great company.

Thanks to Jeff for sharing his thoughts. Find him at www.jeffsanders.com

In interviewing Jeff for the book, I also found out that it took three years (there is that answer again) for Jeff to land a sponsor.

Joe Rogan has stated that he won't use a sponsor that he wouldn't personally use.

Mark Bologna of the *Beyond Bourbon Street* podcast knows his audience and what they want. For example, one of his sponsors is a local hotel that has approximately 120 rooms. It has a local vibe to it, and his audience wants a curated, off-the-beaten-path experience. If a big hotel chain wanted to sponsor the show, it wouldn't be a good fit. Mark said, "If I signed a big hotel chain, I would feel like I was selling out."

You know your audience better than anyone. Choose your advertisers wisely.

CREATING A MEDIA KIT

The first thing we must address is that there are two types of kits.

1. A media kit used by people who want to promote you (interviewers, media).
2. A rate sheet that shows you how much it costs to advertise on your show and in what form.

Some people combine the rate sheet and media kit into one item. That is your call. Don Miller of StoryBrand says if you confuse, you lose. The advantage of having everything in one place is you only need to keep track of one item. The disadvantage of having everything in one place is some people don't need that information.

The Media Kit

The media kit might explain what your show is about, the target listener, and—if you have numbers you're not afraid to share—the total number of downloads per episode after thirty days. You can include comments from your audience, as well as numbers on your social media. You are showing how engaged you are with your audience. People in the media are looking to spotlight influencers. Why? Because they want you to talk about their product, service, or media outlet.

Many people have the media kit as a PDF to download, with a separate download with a high- and low-resolution image of your logo for them to use. If you don't give them specific materials, they will pull random stuff off of your social media that you are more than likely going to hate.

A Rate Sheet

An example of a rate sheet may have a list of different types of ads (pre-roll, mid-roll, post-roll) and the cost of each type of advertisement.

It can also include how much to advertise on the website, and how much to advertise in the newsletter and social.

You might list the minimum number of episodes/time to sponsor.

Many people create bundles that incorporate all the above.

You also always want to include your contact information, website, etc. There is nothing worse than a potential sponsor reading your rate sheet and deciding to give you money, but they can't figure out how to contact you.

THE ADVERTISING CONTRACT

You've worked hard, gone through negotiations, and you've agreed on the contract. The advertising contract has *all* the details of the transaction, so everyone knows what to expect and confusion can be avoided down the line. You are making everything transparent.

After naming the parties of everyone involved (the name of the advertising company, the name of the podcast), the contract clearly states the following:

- How long each ad will be
- Where the ad will be placed in the podcast
- How many there will be
- Who is reading the ad (To be specific, you should name who is on the ad

- Run dates—the specific dates listed
- The rate and price. Is this per episode, per download, or a flat rate regardless? If priced per download, is it downloads for a certain period (e.g., thirty days)?
- If the ad will be used consecutive days/weeks/episodes in a row
- If the audio is going to be in the episode forever (sometimes called "baked in") or rotated out
- If social media is included, all the *specifics* of what is expected and which platforms are included needs to be specified
- If there is any reporting, what is included in the report, when will it be provided, and who is creating it
- Whether the numbers being tracked are from the United States only
- If they want the host to talk about the product, how far in advance (before the ad runs) the host can expect to receive the product
- If a "sample read" is needed (so the advertiser can get an idea of what the ad would sound like), the time frame they need to get comfortable reading it
- How to cancel a contract; how much notice is needed to cancel
- The total number of advertisements
- The total investment for the advertiser so everyone is clear
- The due date of the payment and what forms of payment are accepted

Talking Points

You need to determine who is supplying the talking points about the product and how much improv is allowed if the host wants to go "off script" and not do the talking points word-for-word.

Speaking of talking points, you need a clause about mistakes. If someone reads the bullet points wrong, the advertiser may not want to pay for it. You might have it so that there is a "make-good" clause in your contact.

Wrapping Up the Contract Discussion

The advertising contract is there to eliminate any surprises. Everyone knows what is expected and what each person's role is. Some people add a "goal" to their contract to remind everyone involved what the purpose of the contract/ad is, to keep everyone on track. It may be a little awkward, but by spelling out all the details, you know what is expected and can prevent conflicts later on.

CHOOSING A PRICE FOR YOUR ADVERTISING

How do you know what to charge? There are a couple of ways to determine this. For me, I knew right from the start I was NOT using the CPM method. I was charging a flat rate per episode with a minimum purchase of four episodes. This is how the conversation went in my head.

How about $30 an episode? When I thought about this, and all the work of reading the ads, reporting on the ads, and having my audience sit through the ads, this didn't seem like enough. I was not going to take just any old product. I needed an advertiser that fit me like a glove.

How about $60? Then $120, $150. When I kept getting higher, eventually I thought, *Well, wait a minute. I want my sponsor to make more money than they are spending on the advertisement.* If they are spending $400 on advertising, I want them to make more than $400, so they decide to keep advertising.

Eventually, using my conscience and understanding the costs of their products, and how well they fit my customer, I came up with a price I thought was fair and allowed me to sleep at night.

You might consider asking them how much they pay to acquire a customer (customer acquisition cost), as this may give you an idea of their budget. Remember you want to make a win-win situation.

Joe Saul-Sehy of *Stacking Benjamins* (stakingbenjamins.com) makes a great point. Let the potential sponsor say no. "There are many times we come up with a price, and we think it's too high. Let the sponsor say no—because in some cases they will say yes. You don't know unless you ask them."

I mentioned Mark from the *Beyond Bourbon Street* podcast and how he has a local hotel as a sponsor. How did Mark come up with his pricing? Mark did a little investigation and found out what the cost was to stay at the hotel for one night. Mark knew most people that would come to town would book a three-night stay. Mark then used the price for a three-night stay as his starting price. He knew he could sell at least one of those per episode. Mark and the hotel set up a trial period of three months, and at the end of that period, Mark and the sponsor would sit down and go over their figures. If it was unfair to one of the parties involved, then they would renegotiate. If a fair price couldn't be negotiated, then they would stop the advertising campaign.

Mark also has a Facebook community. When an advertising contract is coming up for renewal, he will reach out to his Facebook community to see if anyone has used the sponsor. For example, when he asked his group if anyone had taken a Two Chicks Walking tour, he got seventy-five answers in two days. The best part is Mark brought his sponsors into his group. This way, the sponsor sees all the comments without Mark having to copy and paste. They see the value firsthand.

Pricing Includes More Than Downloads

Another thing a potential sponsor is looking for is your engagement on social media. If someone sends you an email saying nice things about your show, be sure to start a folder or tag that message in Gmail. You can copy and paste them into Microsoft Word, Evernote, etc. You want to keep that social proof for multiple reasons:

1. You can use those as testimonials to the engagement you have with your audience.
2. You can use them as a morale boost on those days when you think nobody is listening.

On computers running Windows, there is a built-in screen snipping tool (search for "snipping tool"). On Macintosh computers, press Command + Shift + 4. This will turn the cursor into a crosshair, allowing you to select which portion of your screen you would like to capture. Use these tools to capture tweets, Facebook comments, reviews in Apple Podcasts, etc.

When we talk about engagement, this could include:

- Followers on social media (Twitter, Facebook, Instagram, or whatever new tool is hot by the time you read this).
- Your email list. This can be huge. As social sites come and go, the one thing YOU control is your email list.
- If you're starting and you don't have any social proof, then don't include it (but get things in place to start building that list and that engagement).

Think Long-Term When Choosing Your Prices

I was at an event where I got to interview a very successful podcaster who has one ad mid-roll in their somewhat short (less than ten minutes) podcast. This made them stick out. It was a quick, direct-to-the-point podcast, with one advertisement in the middle.

I noticed they started making changes to their format. Their show was much longer on certain days of the week. I asked them if they had anyone complain about the change in the format. They hadn't received anything yet but could tell I was not a fan of the longer episodes a few days a week. When I asked what inspired the format change, the answer was that they had already sold out of all their ad spots for the rest of the year, then a family emergency occurred and they needed to make more money. So they increased the number of ads, which made the episodes longer.

Running out of inventory is a great problem to have, but you do need to remember that when you cash that check, there might not be any more money coming in for the rest of the year. Some podcasters will start with a lower price for ads to try and get someone to invest in their show. If this is your strategy, you may want to add some verbiage that the price is an "introductory offer" or something similar, so advertisers know this lower price will not always be the norm.

REAL-LIFE EXAMPLE: GLENN THE GEEK AND THE HORSE RADIO NETWORK

Glenn "the Geek" Hebert (horseradionetwork.com) has run his podcast as a business from day one. I want to share how Glenn handles his sponsorship. If you want to advertise on the Horse Radio Network:

- Glenn must use the product before you become a sponsor. He will not advertise a product he doesn't believe in. Yes, he has turned down money to guard his integrity.
- You need to advertise for more than one month. It takes months to get your brand embedded in the minds of the listeners.
- Glenn PARTNERS with companies he has formed a RELATIONSHIP with and doesn't use the CPM model (it's a flat rate per episode).
- You are not looking to track promo codes. You are looking to increase the knowledge of your brand.
- As part of Glenn's package, he promotes the brand/product on his podcast/website, but also as part of the agreement, he has the sponsor embed a button/player of their show on the sponsor's website. This player makes the brand look more professional

(kind of a "Look at us, we sponsor radio programs"), and Glenn gets more listeners who then follow his content to his website. His goal was to have one of his buttons/players on every major horse website on the Internet. This helped build his brand, and companies are always trying to "keep up with the Joneses," so when one company saw their competitor on Glenn's site, they would then want to do the same.

- Glenn also has the sponsor agree to promote their episodes on social media. In some instances, they are giving Glenn access to their social sites so Glenn could do the posting for them.

- Glenn has the sponsors come on his show to help with content. This is important. For example, a horse publication might come on to talk about the top three stories for the week. You can see how Glenn is always building relationships and partnerships. When the publication comes on his show, they get exposure, Glenn gets content, and Glenn gets paid. For the sponsor, now THEY are building a relationship with the audience (which leads to more sales), and Glenn gets all the credit. When Glenn received an email from a listener stating, "I love when you put the sponsors on the show because it puts a voice to the name," he sent it out to his sponsors.

As a side note, some sponsors don't mind becoming "a little famous" in the horse community and enjoy coming on the show. Some business owners have egos.

HOW DO I FIND SPONSORS?

There are agencies you can work with if you just google "Podcast Advertising Agencies." Many of these want you to have at least 5,000 downloads an episode. I've worked with Heather Osgood at True Native Media (truenativemedia.com), who seemed more adept at working with smaller shows that appealed to more niche products and brands. You can hear my interview with Heather at https://schoolofpodcasting.com/697.

Glenn Hebert has a great strategy that not only makes it easy to find sponsors but also helps you set your pricing. Glenn found the leading print magazine about horses and turned to the back where the advertisements were (you know, the pages with tons of squares, etc.). After all, anyone listed here had an advertising budget.

First, he called the magazine and asked for pricing on the different-sized ads at the back of the magazine. Then he started calling the smaller ads (not the full-page people, as Glenn had twelve listeners at the time). He explained how he had their target audience over at the Horse Radio Network (which at the time was one show). He asked about the results they were receiving from advertising in the back of a magazine, and then quoted them a better price.

Glenn mentioned that in the beginning he didn't go after the "big" sponsors; he went after the mid-level sponsors and "mom and pop" companies so he could build a relationship with them and have them involved with the message. The big giant companies feel his podcast is too small and won't do the extra things Glenn needs. Glenn uses sponsors to answer listener questions all the time. If he gets a question from a listener about a saddle, he brings on his saddle sponsor to answer the question. By bringing the sponsors on the show *in a non-salesy way,* the audience starts to build a relationship with the sponsor, and Glenn gets all the credit.

Another way to find sponsors is to find an event about your subject. Then see who is sponsoring the event (again, these people have a budget). For example at Comic Con (an event dedicated to comic books, anime, fantasy films and TV shows, etc.), there are sponsors who offer pop icon art, wooden ornaments, collectibles, model kits, and more.

WEBSITE AND NEWSLETTER

People ask me, "Do I *really* need a website for my podcast?" The answer is simple: yes. Here is why. As I write this, Apple has over 870,000 podcasts in its directory. Finding your show is getting tougher and tougher. I have a show called the *Podcast Rodeo Show.* If you type in "Podcast Rodeo Show" into the search, it won't come up. This is probably due to its having the word "podcast" in the name. I am ranking against every other podcaster who used the word "podcast" in their title. If you search for "Rodeo" or "Dave Jackson," it will show up. In general, the search results are not great in Apple and Spotify (and I'm assuming the more directories that pop up, the harder it will become to be found).

The worst thing you can say to your audience is "Find me in Apple," or "Find me wherever podcasts are displayed." What are you doing?! You are missing a KEY time to send your audience to YOUR website where they don't have to *find you*, as you have a subscribe button on your website that walks them through how to subscribe. Lastly, if you're doing any Facebook advertising, this can set them up to have your marketing displayed in front of them (as Facebook will know they visited your site).

When you have a website, you have total control over your brand, your message, and how you want those to be displayed. You don't need to spend thousands on web design. You need a decent header graphic to make a good first impression and make sure you have some color scheme going on. I use the Dixie theme from Second Line Themes for my WordPress site. If you need a free theme, GeneratePress has a free version, and the paid version is very affordable.

I once got an advertiser for a podcast I did simply on the look of my website. It was simple, easy to navigate, and looked professional. They never even asked how many downloads I was getting per episode. They knew I had their target audience. I presented a price, and a deal was made. If I didn't have a website, this might not have happened.

Another core value of your website is that it is *the* place for all things *you*. Over the years, social media websites have come and gone, and if you were using MySpace (remember them?) as your main hub, you would be in a world of hurt. You want your website to be your *home base* for all things *you*. Then your social sites are "satellite offices" that point people back to your website.

Website Income

Making money from banner ads on your site does not draw in the revenue it once did, but just because you make less with banner ads doesn't mean you should completely ignore them. If you're using WordPress, there is a great plug-in called ADRotate (a free and paid version) that you can use to easily have advertisers displayed on your site (as well as affiliate links). While this may not generate any revenue, it's a nice tool to have in your arsenal. I have had affiliate sales come through banners I featured on my site.

Your Newsletter

There is a very old saying in the world of Internet marketing: "The money is in the list." The reason they say that is because it's true. I know people like to say email marketing is dead, but it's just not true. The beauty of a newsletter is you can put your products and services a few clicks away from your audience. With a podcast, there are more clicks involved, and often people are multitasking when listening to a podcast. People (hopefully) are not reading their email in the car while they are driving (while they may be listening to a podcast). People use their podcast to get people to sign up for their newsletter—where they can then get them to purchase products and services.

One strategy for growing your email list is having an item called a "lead magnet." This needs to be something that your audience wants. It must bring value. Just asking someone to "sign up for my newsletter" isn't much of a reason. If you don't have a lead magnet, you could say, "Sign up for my newsletter and have the episode notes automatically emailed to you." The act of signing up for a newsletter must have a benefit.

Key ingredients of a lead magnet are:

- Make it easy to consume. Solve ONE problem. You don't want it to be a GIANT PDF the size of *War and Peace*. Solve one problem that they can read in a few minutes and put into action. This way, they can read it quickly and solve their one issue.
- Make sure it is delivered instantly. If your audience signs up now, they will be reading their new lead magnet instantly.
- Make sure there are actionable steps to take included in the lead magnet. This way, they can see the steps and results of following your guide.
- Make sure it has evergreen content. This way, you don't need to keep updating it.
- Make sure it has actual value. Some of the best lead magnets leave the reader thinking, *I can't believe they didn't charge me for this.*
- Make sure it demonstrates your expertise.

Lead magnets usually offer a piece of digital, downloadable content, such as a free PDF checklist, report, eBook, whitepaper, video, cheat sheets, templates, toolkits, etc.

My audience loves gear. They love microphones, recorders, software, etc. I made a gear guide that answered the most common questions. I give it away to people who sign up for my email list. It answers common questions, so I'm doing consulting at night, and now I have a chance to get them to sign up for my membership site. I also have affiliate links in the gear guide, so I earn some affiliate income as well.

If you need help coming up with ideas for lead magnets, check your website stats to determine your most popular posts/episodes. I use the MonsterInsights plugin (podclick.me/monsterinsights) to pull Google Analytics into my WordPress. One of my top posts was about taking phone calls on your podcast. I made a quick lead magnet and grew my list quickly. You should repeat this for your top ten pages.

If you're just starting, Mailer Lite has a free version of their email management tools (podclick.me/mailerlite). I use Sendfox (podclick.me/sendfox), which currently has a one-payment-for-lifetime configuration. ConvertKit (podclick.me/convertkit) has a little more flexibility, with plans starting at $29 a month. Aweber is another good choice with great support (podclick.me/aweber).

Website Bundles

Now you have a podcast, a website, and a newsletter. Another way your website can make money is you can create a bundle for your advertising where it is one price to be in the podcast episode, another (higher) price to be listed in the "Episode notes" on your website, and a third way.

With this approach, you're not asking, "Would you like to sponsor the podcast?" You ask, "Which way would you like to sponsor the podcast?"

7

Affiliate Marketing

Affiliate marketing is where you help sell other people's items. You are given an item (often a unique link or code) that identifies the customer came from you, and you earn a commission for the referral. If you don't have your own product, you can make more income when you match a product that fits your audience like a glove.

One note about affiliate marketing (and you may notice a pattern here). As Missy Ward wrote in her book *Make Money with Your WordPress Blog: Learn How to Monetize Your Blog with Affiliate Marketing,* "This is NOT a get rich quick scheme." Missy is one of the cofounders (along with Shawn Collins) of the Affiliate Summit (the largest affiliate event in the world).

BE CAREFUL WITH YOUR WORDS

For me, I feel I'm humble. I'm honored that people listen to my podcast, and I always find it a little "weird" when someone is in an elevator with me and recognizes me but is too nervous to say hello. I'm just a dude who loves helping people podcast.

I remember talking to a new client, and we were going over the equipment he was going to need. I ask him if he had any. He did. He had more than he needed. When I asked why he bought one piece of equipment when he already owned equipment that did the same thing, he replied, "You said it was cool." Hearing how he had spent a fair amount of cash was when I realized my words have power. He had spent $600 on equipment he didn't need. I felt horrible.

Now when I do gear reviews, I am always sure to point out that if you already have (insert X equipment), you don't need to buy (insert Y equipment). I don't want people spending their hard-earned cash on items they don't need. I am much more specific and clearer on who should and shouldn't buy the equipment.

HUNDREDS OF DOLLARS . . . $1.50 AT A TIME

I produce a podcast called *Logical Weight Loss*. For a year, I promoted the Total Gym. You might remember the informercials with Chuck Norris and Christie Brinkley. At the time, everyone was familiar with those informercials, and I thought I would piggyback on them. I also had a Total Gym, and I liked it. I promoted the product for seven months, and FINALLY someone bought one. I made $75. However, if you divide that by the twenty-eight episodes I had put out in the seven months, it was $2.67 an episode. In looking back, the product was expensive, and the more feedback I got, the more I discovered that my audience was primarily made up of women. Many of these women had smaller children.

I did an episode on Fitdecks. A Fitdeck is a deck of cards where you could deal yourself a workout. I bought a deck (they were $15) and tried them out. I explained how it worked. Each day I got a new workout, and I could feel it working. Then I said a magical phrase that I think ignited my audience: "I could see you using these to make a game, and turn exercise into a game with your kids." Suddenly I started getting emails stating I had earned a commission. There were different types of decks each with different types of exercises. I would make $1.50 a deck. I would get emails stating I had earned $1.50 up to $6.00 multiple times a day. Seeing this instant success, I started treating them like a sponsor and mentioning them and using my own personal experience. I had between 2,000 and 3,000 people listening, and I started getting my monthly affiliate checks, and they were in the hundreds of dollars. How could this be right? After all, I was earning $1.50 a deck! I had found a product that fit my audience, and it fit their budget. I was sad when they turned the physical decks into an app for your smartphone.

I was an early adopter of the Fitbit products. I would earn nine dollars every time one was sold. As these were new to the world, there was quite a bit of buzz around it. I would ask my audience what their Fitbit name was so we could be friends and challenge each other. This activity may have ignited FOMO for my audience (the fear of missing out). When I did the math and calculated the CPM, it was over fifty dollars. Once again, a product that fit my audience, and fit their budget (the original Fitbit that just counted steps was around sixty dollars).

My last story about affiliate marketing revolves around a short podcast I did called *The Jillian Michaels Podcast*. Why? Because Jillian Michaels (famous fitness guru) had stopped doing her radio show (that was published as a podcast) to return to do more seasons of the television show *The Biggest Loser*. Consequently, everyone was looking for Jillian Michaels's podcast, so I made one. Why? First, I'm a fan. I love her no-nonsense approach. Secondly, Jillian seemed to be putting her name on every type of fitness product, and they all had affiliate programs (often through Amazon.com, which I will talk about in a bit). She also had books and fitness DVDs.

I wasn't deceitful. I would explain that I wasn't Jillian Michaels (most people figured that out). I explained this was a *fan cast* and I was *not* a representative for Jillian Michaels. I would follow what Jillian was up to on Facebook, talk about information she had in her newsletter, etc. Then Jillian did something she had never done before. She had a new book out, and she was publishing the audiobook where SHE was reading the book. I was an affiliate of audible.com. This program pays me fifteen dollars for every new customer. The pitch to the audience mentioned how this was the FIRST time Jillian was reading her new book, and they could get it for FREE by following my special link. I was very happy when I received my first four-figure affiliate check.

Audible.com is one of the longest running advertisers/affiliates in podcasting. Why? Because we have their target audience (people who like to listen to content). While you can mention that you get your first book for free and the other features of Audible, I found I could make a bump in sales by personalizing the pitch. I was a customer of Audible. I did a podcast for musicians, so when Sammy Hagar, Steven Tyler, and Keith Richards had books come out, I would get them, listen to them, and tease the book to my audience. Here again, I was doing the little thing that not everyone was doing. For me, just getting one or two sales a month would pay for my podcast hosting. The beauty of podcasting is your episodes keep working long after you publish them. I haven't pushed Audible much lately, and I just checked my stats; I earned $75 in the last five months *for doing nothing.* That pitch to get Jillian reading her book is as true today as it was when it first came out. To check out the Audible affiliate plan, go to podclick.me/audibleaffiliate.

TIPS FOR SUCCESSFUL AFFILIATE MARKETING

As someone who has been using affiliate programs for decades, I am here to share what works:

- Everything in podcasting starts with your knowing target audience. This is where Facebook groups, email lists, or any other way (besides your podcast) you can get to know your audience is important.
- Does this product solve a problem for your target audience? Netflix was successful because it solved the "late fees" problem of Blockbuster Video and the "new movies not being in stock" problem of the smaller mom-and-pop video stores. The more the product solves a problem for your audience, the better the chance they will buy it. A great example of a perfect fit is Corey Fineran of the *Ivy Envy* podcast (about the Chicago Cubs) using ParkWhiz as an affiliate. What does ParkWhiz do? According to their website (parkwhiz.com), they "find parking anywhere, for now or for later, compare prices & pick the place that's best for you." Do you know who would use this? People going to a Cubs game, trying to find parking around Wrigley Field in Chicago. It would also help if you're someone who has gone to an away game, and you're in a new city. The product fits his audience and solves a problem.
- Don't go for the product with the largest payout. I told you how I picked the Total Gym due to its high dollar commission. It didn't fit my audience, and I just wasted time. Daniel J. Lewis (theaudacitytopodcast.com) explained how he once mentioned Bluehost (a web hosting company) on his podcast about a television show because it had a large commission. It wasn't relevant to his audience, and he now wants to go back and edit those episodes.
- What products do you use and love? Go to their website and look at the bottom of the website for the word "affiliates" or "partners." If you can't find one (not every company has one), contact the company. For whatever reason, some companies make you ask. Talk about why you love the product from your personal use. Promoting products you

use personally will have more impact (typically) then the built-in bullet points from some marketing plan. I would *strongly suggest* you start with the products you own and use while you are still building trust.

- How easy was it to order and check out at their site? You may find the perfect product for your audience, but their website is a mess. You won't earn any commissions if your audience can't figure out how to buy the product.
- Read their agreement and look for the minimum payout. You might find a great product that fits your audience, but you need to earn $100 in commissions before you get paid.
- If possible, check the affiliate programs statistics. You can often see how successful their program is with stats such as average sale and average conversion (how often people buy).
- If it's possible to see the contact information (in many cases it's not due to privacy laws) of the person who purchased through your link, reach out to them and thank them. Also, be sure to ask them how their experience was purchasing and using the product.
- If you can do this without breaking the terms of service, offer bonus products. In the past, I would offer a free month of the School of Podcasting to anyone who purchased web hosting though my affiliate link. I would then install WordPress for them as well. This strategy tripled the number of affiliate sales. Why did I do this? I had installed WordPress and had automated the steps, so it took me less than ten minutes. If I added the amount of time it took to add them as a student to the School of Podcasting, my total time was fifteen minutes. That means $50 for fifteen minutes of work, or $200 an hour. Also, it allowed potential students to take a test drive of the School of Podcasting. When their free month was over, I would offer a discount code to launch their subscription. You want to check your terms and conditions in the affiliate agreement, as some companies do not want you using this strategy.
- Honest to God, I'm not making this up. I was at an event and ran into a representative from Awin (awin.com), one

of the largest affiliate networks, and I asked what some of the biggest mistakes affiliates were making. Her answer? Publishers forget to put the affiliate link in the post.

• Choose one affiliate in a product type. For example, you lose credibility (or at least cause confusion) when you say, "Use Cooler Websites for your website" and then later say "Or Sitegound." Pick one and be confident in your recommendation.

Amazon.com

Amazon.com sells everything. They are huge, and that is why they are getting their own mention in this chapter. Each month more than 197 million people around the world get on their devices and visit Amazon.com. That's more than the entire population of Russia. In 2018, Amazon's share of the US ecommerce market hit 49 percent. That's 5 percent of all retail spending across the entire country. Here is the kicker: 95 million people in the United States have Amazon Prime memberships.

If you learn nothing else from this book, learn this: Read the Amazon terms and agreement. They are confusing, and if you break them, you will be kicked out of the program. I was kicked out of Amazon's program, and at the time I thought, no big deal. I had pages that had podcasting gear that brought in hundreds of dollars a month. I took that page and swapped out the affiliate links for a different company that was respected in audio and video (bnh.com), with the same copy, photos, etc. I watched my affiliate income almost disappear. It went from three figures to two. People are *very* comfortable ordering from Amazon and with their Prime memberships they don't hesitate at all to click the buy button. Other companies don't have this advantage.

Here are some things you should know (and again, read Amazon's entire thing when you sign up). I want you to see how tricky this can be.

You MUST put the phrase "As an Amazon Associate, I earn from qualifying purchases" on your website. I put the phrase in the footer of my website, so it was always visible. Their terms also have a phrase: "Except for this disclosure, you will not make any public communication with respect to this Agreement or your participation in the Associates Program without our advance written permission. You will not misrepresent or embellish our relationship with you (including by expressing or implying that we support, sponsor, or endorse you), or express or imply any affiliation between us and you or any other person or entity except as expressly permitted by this Agreement."

I was once kicked out of the program because I had the phrase "Support the show" above an Amazon image. You can't mention how it helps the show, etc. Some of you might be saying, "But Joe Rogan does this!" As I write this, Joe has an Amazon button on his page at joerogan.com that says "SUPPORT THE PODCAST SHOP HERE." In the same way your mother said, "If Jimmy Johnson jumped off the roof, would you?" I need to remind you that just because Joe does it doesn't mean it's a good idea (and it often appears famous people have a different set of rules).

Another interesting phrase is "The term of this Agreement will begin upon your registration for or use of the Associates Site. Either you or we may terminate this Agreement at any time, with or without cause (automatically and without recourse to the courts, if permitted under applicable law), by giving the other party written notice of termination provided that the effective date of such termination will be 7 calendar days from the date notice is provided."

The phrase that catches my eye there is *without cause*. Do your best to follow the results, but even if you follow the rules, they can terminate you without cause.

You also can't have any link with the word *amazon* or a variant of *Amazon*. Some people tried putting a subdomain such as amazon.yourwebsite.com. The next time their audience went to type amazon.com, they often would see the subdomain they previously used. This strategy is against the rules.

Here is another tricky one: "Because prices for and availability of Products that you have listed on your Site may change, your Site may only show prices and availability if: (a) we serve the link in which that price and availability data are displayed, or (b) you obtain Product pricing and availability data via PA API and you comply with the requirements regarding use of PA API in the License."

This means you can't put the price of the product. You can use their picture that shows the price, but you shouldn't put the actual price in the text on your website (as it can change).

I love the plugin for WordPress called Pretty Links. However, according to Amazon:

(v) You will not cloak, hide, spoof, or otherwise obscure the URL of your Site containing Special Links (including by use of Redirecting Links) or the user agent of the application in which Program Content is displayed or used such that we cannot reasonably determine the site or application from which a customer clicks through such Special Link to an Amazon Site.

Need a translation? Geni.us (a cool tool for affiliates) states the following about the above paragraph:

> This line from the Amazon.com Associates Operating Agreement just states that you cannot use links that obscure the referring site, preventing Amazon from seeing where clicks originated. Geniuslink conforms to this by preserving the referrer information and passing it on to Amazon with each click.

Amazon goes on:

> (w) You will not use a link shortening service, button, hyperlink, or other ad placement in a manner that makes it unclear that you are linking to an Amazon Site.

Here again, I turn to Geni.us, a company who has been working with these guidelines for years. On their website, they state:

> Associates aren't allowed to frame the Amazon site with any other URL, so if the links you build don't resolve to the www.amazon.com domain in the address bar, you cannot use them in the Associates Program. You will also want to carefully review your links to ensure your Associates tracking ID is included when the shortened URL resolves to the Amazon page. Additionally, because of the way shortened URLs function, Amazon may ask you to provide the specific sites on which the shortened URLs are posted and to make any social network profiles on which you post these URLs publicly accessible for verification purposes.

As I said before, set some time aside and go over the entire agreement. Amazon's commissions (fees) go from 4 percent of the sale up to 10 percent. An example might be if someone purchased a musical instrument for $175 and their fee/commission was 6 percent, you would earn $10.50.

If you join Associates (the name of their affiliate program), be sure to install the Amazon Site Stripe. When you are looking at any page on Amazon.com, you can quickly get the official Amazon link (with or without the image). It's a huge time-saver.

I will say Amazon's support for Amazon Associates is good. I've called and gotten a person on the phone. If you're confused, give them a call. Remember, there is a good chance the terms have changed since this book was published.

If you want to do a deep dive into Amazon and you're using WordPress, you might look into the EasyAzon plug-in, which makes it super easy to make links, AND you can sign up for International Amazon Associates and earn commissions from traffic to your site from other countries. The plug-in identifies which country the visitor is from and uses the appropriate link. You can look at your stats in most podcast platforms and see where your audience is located. Be sure to sign up as an Amazon Associate in those countries. While it may not be an additional major amount of money that comes from these additional countries, you will see where the key to making money with podcasting is having multiple streams of income.

Amazon also has an official WordPress plug-in that is getting better as time goes on.

One last point on Amazon. Don't put all your eggs in their basket. I love Amazon, but I've been kicked out of their program, and there is no appeal process. Also, in the past, they've changed their commission rates with no warning. In other words, don't make plans to pay your car payment with your Amazon payments. It may just go away.

Affiliate Networks

Affiliate networks are resources where you can find many different products. The bonus of a network is it makes it easier to get paid. If your minimum payout is fifty dollars, you might earn ten dollars from one affiliate program, twenty-five from another, and another fifteen from a third product. Normally none of these commissions would be enough to pay out, but networks combine them, and you end up with money quicker than doing a solo program from a vendor. Here are some things to think about when you want to give affiliate marketing a try.

Be Honest and Stay Legal

Always disclose your affiliate connection when talking about products on your website or podcast. The FTC requires that you disclose when you're using affiliate links; in general, it's just the right thing to do. Here is a quote from the FTC website:

Say you're planning a vacation. You do some research and find a glowing review on someone's blog that a particular resort is the most luxurious place he has ever stayed. If you knew the hotel had paid the blogger hundreds of dollars to say great things about it or that the blogger had stayed there for several days for free, it could affect how much weight you'd give the blogger's endorsement. The blogger should, therefore, let his readers know about that relationship[1].

Per their guidelines, it needs to be crystal clear. They state on their website: "Consumers might not understand that 'affiliate link' means that the person placing the link is getting paid for purchases through the link. Similarly, a 'buy now' button would not be adequate."

So, you need to have a disclosure stating that some links on your website may result in your getting paid for mentioning the product.

Recently I reviewed the Rode RØDECaster Pro. It's a great mixer/recorder/ headphone amp/jingle player in one. When I did the review, I shared that Rode had lent me a unit to use. I explained why I liked the unit, but I also mentioned the things I wished they would change in the future (and to their credit they did). You might be tempted just to say positive things to encourage people to buy the product you are talking about, but that is shortsighted. If someone buys a product and it doesn't work as well as you described, you lose your credibility and integrity. It can be very hard or in some cases, impossible to get it back.

My "It's not perfect" review of the RØDECaster resulted in eleven sales and $131 in commission.

AFFILIATE JARGON

You will see all sorts of jargon when it comes to affiliate marketing and affiliate networks. Let me help you sort out some of the acronyms.

- CPA affiliate programs (cost per acquisition)
- CPS (cost per sale)

---

1   "The FTC's Endorsement Guides: What People Are Asking," Federal Trade Commission, last updated September 2017, https://www.ftc.gov/tips-advice /business-center/guidance/ftcs-endorsement-guides-what-people-are-asking #affiliateornetwork.

- CPC (cost per click)
- CPM (cost per 1,000 impressions)

Most of the products I promote are CPS (where I only earn a commission if a visitor buys something). I don't see too many people using CPC and CPM, as it might be easy to have bots fake traffic and clicks. You may be confused about why there are both CPA and CPS; in my world, they are the same. When someone buys a product, the merchant acquires the customer. I'm sure some marketing/affiliate nerd could explain it better, but for me—in my world— they sure seem to be the same thing. When someone buys something using a code or link that identifies that the customer came from me, I get paid.

STRATEGIES FOR AFFILIATE MARKETING
Joint Ventures

Say you find a product that you love, or you know your audience will love. We are going to return to a common theme in this book: start building a relationship with the brand. The goal is to partner with the brand. Start thinking about strategies where both you and the brand can win.

One example of this is John Lee Dumas. John does the show *Entrepreneurs on Fire* (eofire.com) and is hugely successful. John's target audience is entrepreneurs who are trying to create a business. In a course on createlive.com, John mentioned how he worked with Leadpages (a product that would fit in nicely with John's target audience). He put together a webinar to learn more about Leadpages. The webinar wasn't a giant sales pitch (but as is the case with every webinar, there was more than likely a special deal for people on the call).

John has a *huge* audience, and 989 people signed up to attend the webinar. WHOA! you might say. There is a little something called the "rule of 3 percent," which shows that any time you need your audience to take action, you can expect 3 percent of them to do it, if you are doing really well. John's audience went above and beyond: 312 people actually showed up to attend the webinar (33 percent), and of those who attended, 137 purchased the product. Those 137 sales represent 14 percent of the original audience (a testament to John's influence).

The product was $997, and John was making a 50 percent commission. Fifty percent of $997 is $498.50. If you multiply that by the 137 who purchased the product, that would be $68,294.50. You need to keep in mind that the replay of that webinar will bring in additional income. John found the right product that fit his audience, and the payoff was huge.

Other benefits include the cross-promotion John received from the brand promoting the webinar, as some of their audience may be interested in John's products (podcasting, webinars, productivity).

We will talk tools in another chapter, but this is where you need to think long-term. Yes, when you first start, fifty dollars for a webinar platform may seem like a large investment, but when you match the right product to the right audience, you can have great results.

I'm not sure how I missed this strategy myself, but I will be doing these in the future.

The Quick Product Demo

This strategy is simple, and the ultimate in passive income. One of the things that can boost affiliate sales is the trust your audience has in you. When you demonstrate how much you know about the product, this can boost sales that run on autopilot.

Both Michael Hyatt (michaelhyatt.com) and Pat Flynn (smartpassiveincome.com) have videos that show you how easy it is to install WordPress on a certain web hosting company. This starts with knowing your audience (that seems to be a theme here). What if your audience wants to start their own business, but they don't know a thing about building a website? The videos that Michael and Pat created demonstrate how with just a few clicks your website could be built, and if you've used Microsoft Word, then using WordPress is not too far a leap. Just click the link (affiliate link) below the video. One last note about Pat and Michael—both had WordPress themes custom designed for their audience and sold them as their own product.

In looking at Pat's income report, I see his video made $27,650 in affiliate income.

I used a similar strategy where I did a quick demo of a product called Text Expander during one of my webinars (podclick.me/textexpander). This resulted in a quick $378. Why did this work?

- It fit my audience.
- It fit their budget.
- I showed examples of how I use it.
- I made it super clear where to click to get more information.

Now, what if you did this with every product you love?

Reseller

What is the difference between a reseller and an affiliate? It can be a bit confusing. I will use my example of GoDaddy. GoDaddy is a company that provides domains, web hosting, email, SSL certificates, and many other products around websites. Their affiliate payout is between 10 and 15 percent.

Web hosts often give big commissions on web hosting. Why? Because most people don't switch from web host to web host too often. When you deliver a new customer, there is a good chance they are going to stick around a while. Previously I was making $99 for a new referral to Hostgator (more on that later). As much of my audience already had a web host, these would come in now and then. Then I investigated being a reseller for GoDaddy.

The cost to be a reseller is around $180/year. In return, I can purchase domain names, web hosting at (almost) cost. I have A LOT of domain names and A LOT of websites. I am my own top customer. The money I save on websites, domains, etc. easily pays for my reseller fee. However, I can also turn around and sell my audience domains and websites, and everything GoDaddy offers.

With zero promotion (outside of a few links in blog posts), I had 164 orders, resulting in a four-figure commission. I would have to sell ten to twenty web hosting packages (depending on the affiliate payout) to make that much income. I bring up reselling as it may make more sense for you to be a reseller than an affiliate. You do get reports on what people are buying. I also can make coupons for my VIP groups.

Make a Resource Page

If there are products that go along with your topic, make a resource page. I have a resource page that shows what equipment I use, what tools I use, where I host my website, etc. Why do you want to do this? Your audience wants to follow in your footsteps. They know, like, and trust you, and consequently trust what you trust. Make a resource page with all the items you use.

Make sure your resource page is shareable. You can use a tool like Click to Tweet (clicktotweet.com) or the Social Warfare plug-in. If you make a great resource page, people will want to share it with their friends.

Skimlinks, the Lazy Affiliate—Money for Almost Nothing

I was originally going to mention Skimlinks in the tools section, but in a way, Skimlinks is more of a strategy. That strategy is, "I'm not interested in grabbing affiliate links, and in general just don't care about affiliate marketing" (or you've been kicked out of Amazon). You can use a website called Skimlinks.

The good news is it's very easy to set up on your site with a WordPress plug-in (or scripts if you're not running WordPress). Skimlinks partners with fifty affiliate networks, to give its editorial team seamless access to 48,500 merchants around the world and the ability to earn a commission from them. On top of that, Skimlinks negotiates exclusive commission rates from merchants for publishers it works with, which generate 49 percent incremental revenue. Merchants include Nordstrom, Sephora, Alibaba, Expedia, and Asos. You can have a Skimlinks account and use it on multiple websites.

If you started out putting your affiliate links on your website, Skimlinks would leave those alone.

The bad news? They take 25 percent of all commissions, and they pay once a month. However, it is a "set it and forget it" solution and handy for those people who (due to Amazon being in their state) are not allowed to be an affiliate for Amazon. I know what you're thinking: *Twenty-five percent!* But stop a second. You originally weren't going to do ANY affiliate networking. That would result in zero percent in affiliate sales. Now with a quick plug-in/script, you are earning 75 percent of your affiliate income.

THE TOP AFFILIATE NETWORKS

I could make a very large list of affiliate networks. There are many networks. I will keep updating this list at profitfromyourpodcast.com/resources.

Amazon.com

I've already mentioned them, but if you can follow the rules of their terms of service, it is handy to be an Amazon affiliate because they sell *everything*. Their minimum payout is ten dollars. If Amazon has a physical location in your state, you can't be an affiliate.

Their website is affiliate-program.amazon.com.

eBay Partner Network

Most of us know eBay. Like Amazon, they sell everything. Like Amazon, they have a minimum payout of ten dollars.

Their website is partnernetwork.ebay.com.

Awin

You might have heard of them as "Affiliate Window"; this network has 13,000 advertisers. This company was founded in Germany, and they have more European merchants (British and EU) than some other networks. They are currently in eleven countries. They have some big names like Etsy. They currently have a bit more focus on financial retail shopping (fashion), sports, beauty, home and garden, and travel products.

Awin is one of the few networks you must pay a fee to apply—five dollars. If you are approved, you get the five dollars back. They pay out twice a month (which is nice, as many networks pay once a month), and their minimum payout is twenty dollars.

Their website is www.awin.com.

Shareasale.com

This network was founded in 2000. Shareasale.com is one of the largest US affiliate networks. It has more than 3,900 merchants. In 2017 Awin (one of the largest affiliate networks on a global scale) purchased them, which has boosted their international opportunities.

It is one of my favorites. See podclick.me/shareasale.

MaxBounty

This network is all about delivering leads to their merchants (CPA: Cost Per Action). You might have a merchant that is looking to grow their email list or in some fashion get more leads. If your audience is interested in market research, real estate, social games, finance, dating, and diet, you might want to check them out. They pay out weekly with a minimum balance of fifty dollars.

Their website is www.maxbounty.com.

Rakuten Affiliate Network

This network is a great alternative for those looking to avoid Amazon as many of the merchants focus on physical goods. They typically offer creatives (graphics, etc.) to help promote the merchants.

Their website is marketing.rakuten.com/affiliate-marketing.

Clickbank

While Rakuten has a lot of merchants who focus on physical goods, Clickbank is one of the longest running networks with a heavy focus on digital products.

They specialize in informational products (ebooks, courses), etc. Clickbank's minimum payout is ten dollars.

Their website is www.clickbank.com.

CJ Affiliate

CJ Affiliate was previously known as "Commission Junction." Some consider this to be one of the largest networks online. They offer global merchants. I do like that they give you the ability to contact the merchants. If I find a product that I really want to promote, I will submit my show for approval and then send an email to the merchant to explain why my audience is a perfect fit for their product. Their minimum payout is fifty dollars.

Their website is www.cj.com.

2Checkout

This network specializes in digital goods, Software as a Service (SaaS), and ecommerce software. Their website states they have more than 22,000 software products and online titles. Recently Avangate merged with 2Checkout.

Their website is www.2checkout.com.

Market Health

This network specializes in health and beauty products. They have a global reach to more than a hundred countries. Their minimum payout is twenty dollars

Their website is www.markethealth.com.

Pepperjam

Pepperjam strives to get affiliate and merchants working together. Everyone is invited to meet direct and network at a conference once a year. They have a fair amount of coupon activity and digital products. Their minimum payout is twenty-five dollars.

Their website is www.pepperjam.com.

FlexOffers

This is a newer directory that features some bigger companies (Hulu) as well as up-and-coming companies like Powtoon. Their website states over 12,000 merchants are offering a wide variety of programs. If you're looking for a personalized approach, you get your own affiliate manager to help you get the most out of your affiliate marketing efforts. FlexOffers pays its publishers every month on net sixty terms. This means that commissions earned during the month of March (1–31) are processed sixty days later on May 30.

Their website is www.flexoffers.com.

THE DOWNSIDE OF AFFILIATE MARKETING

Keep in mind that as a podcaster, you start with two things:

- No listeners
- Integrity

When you align your brand with another brand as an affiliate, you are "endorsing" that brand. I did this for a decade at a web-hosting company. I used them. I loved them. Their support was amazingly fast. They were purchased by a company, and slowly I started seeing their support become slower and slower. The services their support was happy to help with for free started becoming something I had to pay for (malware removal). Eventually one day I had an issue with one of my sites and the person on the chat (that I had waited close to forty minutes to chat with) was going through a script and, in the end, didn't solve my problem. Whenever I was asked whom I used, I would answer and refer to this web host and explain how I used them for years hoping they would get their act together.

I asked a few friends, and eventually tried a few different hosts and landed on GoDaddy. I had hated GoDaddy for years. They seem to want to nickel and dime you to death. I put a few websites on their service, and as you know, it worked so well that I am now a reseller. The tipping point was when they called me to let me know I could save money by changing the configuration in my setup. I hung up for the phone and thought, *That company just made a call to that increased customer satisfaction while decreasing revenue.* I love a company that puts their customers first. Hence, coolerwebsites.com was born.

What Happens If a Company You Are Promoting Starts to Have Problems?

This happened to me with a WordPress theme. It was great. I loved it and promoted it and made a fair amount of commissions. Then the owner disappeared. By that, I mean he said, "I'm taking a vacation in November to be with my family. I'll see everyone next year." He never came back.

The support team/company seemed to be fine. Support questions were answered. Then I noticed that affiliate payments were behind. It had been close to six months since anyone had heard from the owner and emails to him went unanswered. What did I do? I let my audience *know what was going on*. I told them I loved the product, the company seemed fine, but I was worried about the owner. Something seemed a little weird, so buy with caution. Then the support team disappeared. I quit promoting the theme and again told my audience. I updated the links on my website (this is where a plug-in like Pretty Links can be a *huge* time-saver as I had always used a Pretty Link to point to their website) and changed the Pretty Link to point toward my new recommended theme. This meant all the mentions of it on my site were now updated.

I share this story so you can see the warning signs. It has only happened to me once in my twenty-plus years of being on the Internet (thankfully), but you always want to keep your eyes open.

As I mentioned before, Pat Flynn was making five figures a month promoting a web host. Then he started getting complaints from customers of poor service. Pat had been recommending the company for years and was the top affiliate. He used his power. He flew to their headquarters and said, "This can't happen." The company put together an action plan and created a special connection for Pat's audience to get support. He also kept in touch with his audience via social media and took pictures of himself at the headquarters. This transparency took Pat's credibility score even higher, and he continues to promote the web host today.

HOW TO PICK AN AFFILIATE NETWORK

I often will come to a network after finding a product I like, and then clicking on a link at the bottom of their site labeled "affiliates." This leads me to the network they use to manage their program. This is where knowing your audience comes in handy.

If I *know* my audience will love this product, I might sign up even if they have a higher minimum payout (as my audience will get me to the higher payout). However, if I start to look around, and the dashboard is confusing, and their reporting is messy, this may lead to headaches in the long haul.

If I find a new product that I'm interested in, and they are part of a network where some of the other products I look at are somewhat spammy, I see that as a red flag. I think we've all experienced this with movies. You watch four boring trailers on the DVD, and then you're not surprised when the feature movie is bad.

The worst experience I've had with networks (besides getting kicked out of Amazon) was JVZoo. They specialize in digital products. Some of them were very good, and they have a nice newsletter to announce new products. I was doing a podcast called *Weekly Web Tools* and often would purchase and then spotlight these products on my show and earn commissions.

There is a common phrase on the Internet: "Marketers Ruin Everything." This was the case with JVZoo. I would find out about these great products and promote them to my audience, only to have the product taken off the market after a limited time. This was done intentionally by the seller to create a sense of urgency. The problem is I would have a listener listen to an episode three months later and go to purchase the product and find that it wasn't available. This started to happen regularly.

It wasn't always bad. I looked at my account, and I saw where I earned money. Over the years I used the platform, my lowest commission was $3.70 for a package of royalty-free images; my highest was $591 for a product called the Podcast Interview Wizard (which was helpful in brainstorming and doing interviews on a podcast).

At one point, I used them as my affiliate program, and again, their interface was clunky. Paying and tracking affiliates was a bit of a mess. I never really got any sales from the network of affiliates and moved my membership site to Thinkific, which had its own built-in affiliate program (and I get more referrals from my students/members than I ever did from people on the network).

The JVZoo interface was a bit clunky, and they didn't help me when I sold two products, and the seller never paid me. They also started advertising on their dashboard. I found this tacky. I'm trying to see if I've had any sales, and I need to scroll past your announcement of some contest and how MY PRODUCT COULD BE HERE.

All that is to say, looking back, it just wasn't smooth. Most successful networks have put some time and money into the user interface. They *must*, as there are often thousands of merchant programs to choose from, and they must make it easy to be found. Then it must be easy to get links, graphics, etc.

One of the reasons I like Shareasale is when I log in, I see my current balance and my last payment. It alerts me if any of the merchants I'm promoting has low funds (kind of a "yellow light of caution" about a vendor). I can see which programs I am promoting are getting the most clicks, commissions, transactions, etc. If a product I promote has new graphics, there is an area to let me know.

Shareasale also lets me know what holidays are coming up as there might be a season ahead that would fit nicely with my products (and I might want to create content around the season). All this is put together in an easy-to-navigate dashboard.

Most of the larger networks have decent dashboards. If you log in to a new network and it looks like their design was done fifteen years ago, you might want to keep looking. I know we're not supposed to judge a book by the cover, but in my travels, if the dashboard, reporting, and commissions are hard to grasp, you might find yourself wasting your time.

A DEEPER DIVE INTO AFFILIATE MARKETING

If you are having success at affiliate marketing and want to take it up a notch, there is an event held in multiple locations multiple times a year through Affiliate Summit (www.affiliatesummit.com).

There is also a magazine at feedfront.com, which is run by the same people. They also have a podcast, *This Is Affiliate Marketing*, at affiliatemarketing.libsyn.com/podcast.

SUMMARY

- Affiliate marketing can be a good source of income. It's best to start with the products that you use if they fit your audience. As you are earning the trust of your audience, starting with products you use makes it easier to sound natural when talking about the products.
- Always follow the guidelines of the affiliate program and be honest with your audience. Make sure the products you are promoting fit your audience and will deliver value. Even though you didn't create the product, by promoting the product, you are linking your brand with the brand of the merchants.

8

Crowdfunding

Crowdfunding and donations are a great option for those whose niche doesn't tie itself to a product. For example, let's say you do a podcast where you interview people who have "inspiring stories." While people will feel inspired at the end of the episode, there may not be an obvious product, the way a running shoe fits a running-themed podcast. What product goes with inspiration? But there is one very important thing to notice about crowdfunding.

The word is CROWDfunding, not FUNDcrowding. You *need* a crowd. Don't forget that step one is to build your audience. I was listening to a podcaster who thought he was ready for sponsors because he had been podcasting for three years. He was getting three hundred downloads a month (remember, monthly stats are not a good measurement of success). I know it was hard to hear after three years, but unless he had a SUPER NICHE show, three hundred downloads wasn't going to cut it.

THE JOY OF 3 PERCENT

I hear podcasters who have a hundred downloads per episode say, "If I could get 50 percent of my audience to give me $5 a month, that would be $250." While the math is true, the reality is a fairy tale. You're not going to get 50 percent. There is a good chance you won't get 5 percent. I mentioned the rule of 3 percent earlier. Here is a little more on this concept. If you google "Kelvin Ringold 3 percent," you will see:

- The percentage of people who act at a seminar—3 percent
- The percentage of people who respond to direct mail—3 percent

When you say you're going to get 50 percent of your audience, people are going to think you're on drugs. The typical conversion (people who actually take action) is from 1 to 5 percent of your audience.

When I do the live *Ask the Podcast Coach* show on Saturday morning, 3 percent show up to watch live.

In September 2017, on the episode about Oliver Sipple, the VERY POPULAR podcast *Radiolab*—which has sponsors—was reaching out to the millions of people in their audience for support. They were asking for eight dollars per month. At the time they were at .72 percent of their audience financially supporting the show. The host's goal was to get up to 1 percent. This was a highly successful show (it was mentioned in the hit TV series The Good Place) yet they maintained a realistic goal.

WHEN SHOULD YOU LAUNCH A CROWDFUNDING CAMPAIGN?

People ask if they should launch a crowdfunding campaign with their podcast, and while there are no rules in podcasting, I feel focusing on monetization *first* may be a misstep. The successful podcasters I spoke with launched their crowdfunding campaigns when their audience asked for them. They focused on building an audience *first*, then focused on monetization. Jonathan Oakes of the *Trivial Warfare* podcast talks about how you have to do more than fill up your audience's cup with value. It has to OVERFLOW for them to reach in their wallet and support you.

Crowd First, Monetize Second

Let me explain this with a story.

Bobby wants a puppy. Bobby loves Shih Tzu dogs. He had one as a child and would love to have another one. Bobby doesn't make much money and a purebred Shih Tzu costs quite a bit. So, what does Bobby need?

He needs money.

What does Bobby do?

He spends time going to the pet store, looking at all the toys for dogs.

He looks at all the hair accessories and brushes.

He spends money on dog-grooming classes as he wants to be prepared.

He spends time looking at all the great beds in wonderful colors.

He spends a night on the Internet researching the best dog food.

He spends a *lot* of time watching Shih Tzu videos on YouTube.

He spends some time going over the collars and leashes, figuring out which one would be the best for his dog someday.

For me, this is a bit like Patreon (a popular crowdfunding platform). Patreon is a great platform for those who have an engaged crowd. It is, after all, a crowdfunding platform. I see people spending huge amounts of time agonizing about what perks to fit at what levels. They get disappointed at the lack of patrons signing up. They might even quit doing their podcast. If you were to look at their activity, a LARGE amount of time was spent in their Patreon dashboard (not because it's hard to set up, but because it is what they are focused on) when they should be focused on growing their audience. Meanwhile, they just published episode four.

What *should* Bobby do?

If Bobby had taken all the time he spent at grooming class, at the pet store, researching dog food, watching YouTube, looking at leashes, toys, and more, he could have:

- Delivered pizzas
- Driven for Uber, etc.

Bobby would've had enough money to buy his dog.

Step one of having a dog is *get a dog*.

Step one of crowdfunding is *get a crowd*.

If Bobby had taken steps to get the money, he would have a dog. Then he could add these other things later. He might be able to go to a thrift store and get them much cheaper. Then in the meantime, he would have the love and joy of having a dog. The joy that the dog brings him would inspire him to save money and get those extra items because the dog was worth it.

A podcaster could start because they have a passion and love talking about their subject. If they deliver value, they may receive feedback, make connections, and start to build a community. They could buy their gear on eBay. This community fuels them until the community is large enough to monetize. I know two podcasters who have had new computers purchased for them by their audience. Instead of spending tons of time trying to monetize to nobody, they could be spending that time creating AMAZING content that would inspire their listeners to tell a friend.

While there are plenty of people who say, "I don't have the money," there are many who say that while they are sipping their Starbucks coffee. I used to drink two 20-ounce bottles of Mountain Dew a day at work ($1.50 each).

That adds up to $60 a month. If money is so tight that the $30 a month it takes to run a podcast will potentially stop you from paying your bills, get a job—not a podcast. You pay for things with one of two things: time or money. Whichever one you have the most of, use for currency.

Patreon has said on their blog that you can expect 1 to 5 percent of your audience will become patrons. So, if you have an engaged audience of 100, expect three-ish people to sign up. If you're doing it for the sole purpose of making money quickly, don't. Let me save you some time. Don't. It just doesn't work that way. Sure, some people say that you can make money from day one. Those are the people who put generic ads on your show that pay (not making this up) .0017 cents per download. If you are lucky enough to have 300 downloads, you will make fifty-one cents.

For me, setting up a Patreon page when you don't have an audience is like fertilizing the ground when you haven't purchased the flowers. It's buying the Hershey's chocolate syrup when you don't have the ice cream. It's buying the peanut butter and jelly when you don't have the bread. (Okay, I think you get my point.)

I know what you're going to say: "But you miss every shot you don't take." To this I say: "You're not in the game yet."

PATREON.COM

Patreon.com is the top crowdfunding platform. The name comes from the early days where people would be a "patron of the arts." You might think of them as a sponsor of their favorite artists. While crowdfunding sounds cool and trendy, in a nutshell, Patreon is a membership platform.

There are three different fees at Patreon:

- **Platform fee:** This is a percentage of a payment to you. These fees range from 5–12 percent, depending on which plan you have.
- **Payment processing fees:** Payment processing fees cover the cost of processing payments from your patrons. If your payment is $3 or less, the fee is 5 percent + 10 cents. If your payment is more than $3, the fee is 2.9 percent + 30 cents. If you are outside the United States, there is an extra 1 percent charge.
- **Payout fees:** These are charges for moving funds from your creator balance to your bank, PayPal, or Payoneer account.

These range from $0.25 (if you are receiving payment via direct deposit) up to $20 (if you are receiving a payout via PayPal outside the United States).

If you want the membership tier, there is an 8 percent fee. To give you an example: if someone pledges $5, Patreon is going to take 8 percent (40 cents) plus processing fees (2.9 percent +30 cents = 45 cents), which means you take home $4.15.

Comparing this to Apple, which takes up to 30 percent for things sold in their apps store, and YouTube can be even more aggressive. The key with any platform is you are paying for convenience. You may find that you can put together your own "Patreon"-type operation using some WordPress plug-ins and PayPal, but the extra time and effort you put into this may not be worth the additional income you earn.

In a video released by Patreon, they stated they have over 100,000 creators. In 2017 they processed $150 million in payments to those creators.

Insights from Top Earners on Patreon

You will see in this chapter that some people are having great success with Patreon. You may be facing that negative voice in your head as you contemplate starting a crowdfunding campaign. You will hear this again and again throughout this book. People who successfully monetize their podcast have a deep understanding of their audience. With Patreon, you need to know what will motivate them to give you money. You also need to know what will keep them engaged.

If you understand your audience well, describing a typical audience member should be easy. This description would include where they are in life, why they enjoy your content, and what kind of resources they can offer to support you.

Here are some questions Patreon feels you need to know the answer to:

- How niche is your content? The more niche (focused) your content on a topic, the smaller the audience—but the more engaged and loyal.
- Why should your audience pay to support you when so many others are doing something similar for free?

That second question is tough to answer, and can result in some people folding up their tent and going home. Their point is you can do a show about health and fitness. Then you could niche down to health and fitness for people over fifty. Then you can niche down again to fitness for men over fifty. You can start niche, generating buzz, as people will feel, "Oh WOW, this show is for ME." Now the answer to the question of "Why should I pay you for your content?" is because you can't get it anyplace else. Then later, after you build your audience, you can expand.

Lee Silverstein produced the show *The Colon Cancer Podcast*. He built a loyal audience and now has expanded it to *We Have Cancer* (wehavecancer-show.com), which can still talk about colon cancer, but also can approach subjects regarding how cancer affects everyone involved with the disease.

- Do people care if *you* are making the content, versus someone else?
- Do you differentiate your work though unique delivery or personality?
- Does your project have a reputation for superior quality?
- Do you have an emotional or personal connection with your audience?
- Do you interact with your audience regularly? (How many fans can you name?)

These questions bring your brand into focus. I've had people say the success of *School of Podcasting* is my personality. I make what can be boring data fun and educational. I have used personal stories to make points on the current subject; at times it takes courage to be vulnerable. This has led to a stronger bond with my audience.

People hear about an engaged audience. This might bring up mental pictures of you tweeting at 2:00 a.m. and never sleeping. This can be as simple as replying to comments, emails, tweets, etc. If your audience reaches out—you MUST reach back. Also, when they reach out to you to ask a question, answer the question but ask *them* a question and start a conversation.

Why People Become Patrons

While there are multiple reasons, the top two reasons are:

1. Support motivated: Your audience wants to give you the freedom and independence to do your art.
2. Benefit motivated: These are the people who are looking for more from you, and they are super excited about these items.

What patrons are looking for:

1. Insights into the creative process
2. Bonus content that they can't get anyplace else
3. Engagement
4. Exclusive merchandise
5. Fan recognition
6. Input on the content

Nearly 40 percent of successful creators reward their patrons with bonus or exclusive content. This makes sense as the exclusive content is content you can't get anyplace else (which increases its value), and bonus content is great for those patrons who want more of your content.

Twenty percent of creators use Patreon's Early Access to give their die-hard fans access to the content before the general public. Mark Bologna of *Beyond Bourbon Street* provides a glimpse of future episodes.

Fifteen percent of creators are sending out physical rewards. Physical rewards are not a new idea. The Beatles fan club would send out buttons and stickers for true fans to help identify themselves. You need to be careful, as your audience is global and fulfilling physical goods can take a lot of time and effort—and you may find out it costs five dollars to ship a 99-cent sticker across the planet. Alan Sisto of *The Prancing Pony Podcast* (theprancingpony-podcast.com) mentioned that sending a sticker overseas is not that expensive because it's flat. However, sending a button overseas might cost fourteen dollars.

Another tip from Alan about physical items is to have a default item. For example, at the five-dollar value, you might get a sticker or a button. Alan recommends stating in the verbiage that if the patron doesn't specify, they get a sticker. Having a default item reduces the amount of time it takes to manage your patrons. According to a post on Patreon.com, when pricing your benefits, use this simple equation: Pricing = Impact + Effort. The price of your benefit should represent the effort you put in *and* the impact for the patron.

Ten percent of successful creators are using Patreon polling options to reward their passionate patrons while also gaining insight into their audience. Getting their opinion via polls helps them feel like "part of the team."

Five percent of successful creators use recognition tools to give a shout-out to their biggest fans. This might be adding their name to the credits of a video or in album liner notes, or thanking your patrons at live events.

The Prancing Pony Podcast rewards patrons of ten dollars or more by moving their questions to the front in their mailbag segment. If you give *The Prancing Pony Podcast* twenty dollars a month you receive some swag, and you get to be involved with a quarterly live broadcast of Q&A. When I interviewed Alan Sisto, he was surprised how much this live event drove people to sign up for the twenty-dollar tier. This shows again that some people want to be involved in the process. The people at their fifty-dollar tier get to pick the topics for the live event (and are part of the recording).

Mark Bologna of the *Beyond Bourbon Street* (beyondbourbonst.com) podcast also answers patrons' questions first on his show and gives them a peek at future episodes. He is currently working on a book with a national publisher and will eventually use an autographed copy of the book as a reward.

Don't Forget the Value and the Clock

You can create exclusive bonus content, but if it doesn't deliver value *to the patron,* then they are not going to stay around a while. You should never hear the phrase "Well, it's only going out to the patrons—not the whole audience" come out of your mouth. You need to stop right there. You are taking your patrons for granted. These people are your sales force. Give them phenomenal content, and they will tell their friends.

Before you go promising to double the amount of content you create, remember you still have a job (probably) and might have a spouse and/or children. Doubling the number of episodes requires you to double the amount of time it takes to create them (unless you outsource some of it). My point being, you get hypnotized by the thought of additional funds, and you end up giving your life away.

Best Practices

1. Offer exclusivity
2. Create a community through naming patron groups
3. Appeal to the masses
4. Provide short- and long-term incentives
5. Provide fan recognition at every tier
6. Provide recurring value through your benefits

I want to talk about number 5 (provide fan recognition at every tier). I have a tier on my Patreon that you get a shout-out in every episode at the twenty-dollar value. When I first started, I felt bad for the other tiers who had not pledged as high. This was a mistake. I should've have given them a shout-out when they joined and welcomed them publicly (or whatever ceremony/traditions you create). Instead, I decided once a month I would read everyone's name and website. After all, I didn't have that many patrons—yet.

Fast forward, and the list grew, and now thanking everyone takes up a fair amount of time in my episode. I recently announced that starting next year you will get a BIG shout-out when you join, but per my original tiers, only twenty-dollar patrons will be mentioned in the show.

I see and hear about this mistake a lot. Call it impostor syndrome, but many of us are not sold on the idea of listeners pulling out their cash for the value we have provided to them. Be patient and over-deliver the value, so they feel moved to support you.

Get Creative with Naming Your Tiers

Naming each level of your membership helps build community. For example, everyone contributing three dollars a month has a group name, as do the five-dollar members, the ten-dollar members, and so on. My largest tier for my Patreon is exclusive (only one person is allowed in this tier) and has bonus content (they get one-on-one consulting) at a discounted rate (adding more value). That tier is rarely ever empty for long. I call that tier the Teacher's Pet.

Get creative and tie them in with your topic. For example, the *Prancing Pony Podcast* (a podcast about Tolkien) has the following tiers:

- $2: Rohan's Reward
- $5: The Gift of Gondor
- $10: The Legacy of Lothlórien
- $20: Elrond's Honorarium
- $35: Bombadil's Bequest
- $50: Círdan's Contribution

Even their descriptions have the flavor of Tolkien. Their two-dollar tier description: "The courtesy of your hall is generous indeed! You have our thanks and genuine appreciation and will be included on our website's Eglerio! page (unless you prefer to be anonymous). You will also receive access to patron-only updates, so you can see what we're working on. Forth Eorlingas!"

When they promote their patron in their podcast, they can explain how you can join the "Fellowship of the Podcast."

Keeping Things Simple Can Work as Well

As is always the case with podcasting, people love to try different strategies. One of the highest earning podcasts on Patreon is *Chapo Trap House* (a political podcast), which offers one tier (five dollars) and the reward is bonus content. Currently, *Chapo Trap House* has over 34,547 patrons making $155,074 per month.

Goals for Your Crowdfunding

Remember that the goals of your crowdfunding should benefit your audience. I've seen things like, "If we make fifty dollars a month, I will buy a new mixer and microphone." Unless your audio is *bad,* that isn't a reward for the audience. It is a reward for you.

Your patrons want to know more about you. You are their leader, their hero, their friend. They want to know more about you, and they want more content. When I looked at the top people on Patreon, it seemed like the top reward was more content. For my own Patreon account, I record an extra thirty minutes, and if you are a patron, you get access.

Get the Ball Rolling with Special Offers

Special offers at Patreon are perks of some sort that are only available for a limited time. This can trigger people (especially super fans) with the fear of missing out (sometimes abbreviated FOMO). Patreon gives you the tools to have limited-time offers. Here are some examples.

One way to get people to become a patron is to explain what they may be missing. Marshall Short has a Patreon where he designs art for role-playing games. He invited his audience to comment on his patron posts to help him decide what to draw next. After all the suggestions had been made, he let them vote on which one to create first. These were seasonal drawings and would only be available during that season. His audience signed up to help influence his choices. This resulted in a $648/month increase.[1]

---

1   Kate Holt, "Artist Turns Authentic Exclusivity into Special Offer Success," *Patreon Blog,* November 14, 2018, https://blog.patreon.com/artist-turns-authentic -exclusivity-into-special-offer-success.

Paul M. Sutter had a book that he had been working on. He stated that anyone who joined at ten dollars per month or higher and stayed for three months (which ensured his costs were covered) would get an autographed copy of the book. He ended up with $553 more PER MONTH.

Rebecca Loebe is a singer/songwriter who saw an increase in 23 percent in monthly earning by creating a unique enamel pin for anyone who joined her five dollar per month tier. This was only available for two weeks.

Beware of Contests on Patreon

With every platform you use, ALWAYS read the terms (they are boring, but you want to follow the rules). With Patreon, they state, "We don't allow raffles, or other games of chance, on our platform because we want to protect creators, patrons, and Patreon. The legality of chance-based contests can differ depending on what country or state you live in. For instance, in the United States, the IRS views raffles as a form of gaming (aka gambling). This means that not only would a raffle be subject to the legal constraints of gambling nationally, but it also may not even be legal in the state you, or your patrons, live in."[2]

Does this mean you can't have giveaways? Their site states:

> Running other forms of contests on Patreon is allowed as long as
> they fulfill the following qualifications:
> * Winning the contest doesn't depend on luck/chance
> * A patron's chance of winning can't be increased by paying more money (like by pledging at a higher tier)

Some People Are Making Boatloads of Money on Patreon

There are some people who are absolutely raking in the cash.

According to Graphtreon (graphtreon.com), the *Chapo Trap House* podcast makes $155,074 per month from 34,547 patrons. The show is political. They launched their crowdfunding in May 2016.

The *Last Podcast on the Left* podcast earns $59,026 per month from 11,855 patrons. They launched their Patreon in September 2014.

---

2   Patreon, "Patreon's Stance on Raffles, Lotteries, and Giveaways," May 28, 2019, blog.patreon.com/patreons-stance-on-raffles-lotteries-and-giveaways.

Is your show too explicit and scaring away advertisers? The *Cum Town* podcast earns $49,197 from 10,962 patrons. They launched their Patreon in June 2016.

When I went to graphtreon.com and looked at the top 100 podcasters, donations ranged from $2.40 per month to $7.14 which averages at $4.57. When I looked at the average time for the crowdfunding campaign for the podcasters in the top 100, their campaigns had been going 2.5 years, and if we round that up, they had been going for—you guessed it—three years.

Let's go back to our download numbers of an average of 1,500 and the median of 150. If we take 3 percent of 1,500, that's 45 people; if we take 3 percent of 150, that's 4.5 people. According to a blog post on Patreon, the average value per Patron (listener) is $7.00 (which is higher than what I saw). This means that averaging 1,500 downloads per episode may lead to an average of $315 per month, and the person with 150 downloads per episode may earn an average of $31.50 per month.

Embrace Your Cause

Sometimes we are worried about voicing our support for a cause or political party. In general, voicing an opinion can be somewhat scary these days. In the words of rock star Jimi Hendrix, "I'm gonna let my freak flag fly." Jack Lowe is on a mission to photo-document all Royal National Lifeboat Institute (RNLI) stations (I think it's safe to say that is pretty niche). Between the United Kingdom and Ireland, there are 238 RNLI stations. For me, born and raised in the United States, there isn't much of an emotional tie. However, if you read his blog at blog.patreon.com/photographer-jack-lowe, it's hard to not want to contribute. The post explains, "Jack has a crowd. He has a group of people who love what he does. Some people in that audience were thrilled to have a new way to support him. He just needed to offer the right method."

Remember that one of the reasons people become a patron is so you can do what you want to do. If what you want to do is a healthy cause, people who may not even know you may support you because they want to support the cause.

JONATHAN OAKES, *TRIVIAL WARFARE*: REAL-LIFE LESSONS FROM PATREON

I got to interview Jonathan Oakes of the show *Trivial Warfare* (trivialwarfare. com). He said:

I started the podcast in February of 2015 and started Patreon in May of 2016.

It was six months of doing the show before we heard from our first audience member via email. I think by the eighth month, we had had four emails from people. We didn't start to experience an audience until January of 2016. [Again, he started in February of 2015.]

When I started our Facebook group, and I was so scared to do that because you're afraid nobody is going to show up and you'll look like a loser. I didn't want to be a loser. The Facebook group was a huge trigger for our first wave of growth. I think it was April 2016 when one of our listeners named Pate Hogan sent an email saying, "I want to buy you guys lunch, the next time you're recording, I want to give you some money. Give me a PayPal email or some way that I can give you money." I gave him a PayPal address, and he sent us like 35 bucks.

I thought, *When you are at the point at which your audience is asking how they can give you money, I should have an answer for that. It should have been easy for the audience.*

That's when the seed was planted because before that, I never considered it. I was spending between $50–$100 a month, and I thought if we could recoup what I'm spending, then that would be great.

While Jonathan did the typical small giveaway items at the lower amounts, he knew that he needed something his audience wanted at the higher levels. He decided his ten-dollar reward was a chance to be on the show.

Jonathan said:

I knew that's what they wanted. Because whenever they sent me emails, or whenever they dropped hints and private messages, or whenever they said something on the Facebook group, they were always saying, I'd love to come on the show, how do I get on the show?

It took me fifty episodes, but I finally figured out how to pull people in the show. I had a ten-dollar level that gave you a chance to be on the show. At the twenty-five-dollar level, you would get to come on the show twice a year. At the fifty-dollar level, you would come on the show four times a year. If you pledge one hundred dollars a year you will come on four times a year, and you would get a microphone, so you sounded good.

Get Creative with Your Levels

Jonathan's fanbase is called the Trivial Warfare Army and occasionally referred to as warheads. Since the fanbase was an army, Jonathan played on the military theme and gave the different Patreon rewards rankings.

- $1: Private
- $3: Sergeant
- $5: Lieutenant
- $10: Captain
- $15: Major
- $25: Lieutenant Colonel
- $50: Colonel
- $100: General

Jonathan said:

This way if the person interacted with the show we could say, "This is Jim who is a captain in the Trivial Warfare Army." That would then give us a chance to then talk about the army. We also bought that domain (trivialwarfarearmy.com) and pointed it at our Patreon page. Having a specific website address makes it super easy to direct people to and get them started. [He also purchased triviawarfarearmy.com for anyone who doesn't hear the L in the name.]

Looking back at that ten-dollar tier, I didn't think anybody would give me ten dollars a month. Ten dollars a month is a lot for something you can have for free.

The first month, we had $99.

The second month, we had $145.

The third month we're at $185.

The next month it was $253.

We didn't have a decrease in earnings month over month for two and a half years.

It was incredible.

The Success Created a Problem

The Patreon campaign was successful enough to the point where after about six months to a year of starting the campaign, Jonathan couldn't keep up with his promises. "When ten dollars gets you on the show once a year, and you have around eighty people sign up, and then thirty people at the twenty-five-dollar tier, which was twice a year, and then another five people who were at the fifty-dollar tier, I did the math and had offered up 230 appearances for a fifty-two-episodes-per-year show."

Those tiers did not work. Jonathan had no concept of how successful his campaign would be. If you ever get a chance to meet Jonathan, he is a great guy, and as you might imagine, this bothered him. He has worked with his community and adjusted some tiers and added more content to help maintain his community (more on that later). Keeping everyone involved and keeping all your commitments is still an ongoing process. While the new level helped, Jonathan said, "I still dealt with stress over not being able to fit in all the people that I'm supposed to fit in, in a year. Currently, we have more than 700 patrons, so I do have a lot of stress around not meeting their needs."

Jonathan's Strategy of Excess Value

In speaking with Jonathan, everything always came back to delivering value. He said:

> Everything that I was doing, and everything that I tried to do was to deliver so much value to my audience that they felt compelled to offer me value back.
>
> Once you have your first person who is starting to tip over and they are saying, "I need to support Jonathan because he has given me so much"—they start to donate. You need to deliver additional value all the time. You do this consistently as you find ways to do more. Creating more value might mean just another episode of the same weekly episodes or bonus episodes or talking to them and becoming their friend. In some cases, you can get involved in doing something special.
>
> I've been asked to do a message for a couple's wedding.
>
> I've recorded proposals for a listener. My advertisement for that week's show (and, no, I didn't charge him for this) was me recording a proposal for this guy who would be listening to the

show while driving over the Rocky Mountains with his girlfriend (now wife).

I was approached by a husband (a warhead) to do a scavenger hunt for his wife. I recorded all the clues for him. His wife had a CD on the seat of her car. When she put it in, it was my voice that came on doing their clues. She's now a good friend.

When you offer them a mechanism to help you—when you're doing so much for them—there is going to be a group of people who take advantage of that.

Two Ways to Increase Your Patreon Income

As we have mentioned, many people become a patron to get more of your material and to support your goals. You can add more content. The other thing you can do to get more pledges is to take something they are getting for free and put it behind a paywall. As you might imagine, taking away something does not always go over well.

Jonathan cared so much about his community and had a built-in focus group (his patrons, his Facebook group), and he talked about changing things with his community. He would still produce the same number of episodes (four per month), but two of them would be for patrons only. If you wanted all four episodes, you would need to become a patron.

In rolling out this new plan, Jonathan made a video that explained his goal of trying to do this full time. Jonathan said, "My biggest fear is I didn't want to break my community over this, and it didn't." I've explained how if you have a truly engaged audience, typically 3 to 5 percent of your audience is going to become a patron. Jonathan is at 7 percent.

Always wanting to deliver value, Jonathan also took the first 150 episodes and put them behind Patreon's paywall, so this was additional content you couldn't get anyplace else.

He also announced a big giveaway to motivate not just new patrons but current patrons to potentially increase their pledge. What did he do? He reached out to one of his listeners who is an artist who designed a T-shirt for the Trivial Warfare Army; it featured your typical nerdlike famous people like Indiana Jones and others. Above this group of people, it reads "Trivial Warfare Army," and under the group, it reads, "I answered the call."

Anyone who either signed up for the five-dollar tier or increased their current pledge got this limited edition T-shirt. It would only be available for the next forty-five days. The logo would be on T-shirts, mugs, mousepads, etc. Jonathan worked with a vendor, so he didn't have to touch any of it. There were also bundles. If you came in at one level, you got the T-shirt. If you came in at another level, you got one of everything. Jonathan explains, "I made it very clear that this was your ONLY chance to get this logo. In the first month, ninety new patrons signed up. Then in the second month, there were one hundred and fifty new signees. Before a final couple of weeks, we added another fifty patrons to the roster. These were new signups during the campaign, and the numbers don't even speak to the number of people who increased their support during the period."

Did everyone love this transition? No, but Jonathan said, "My friends made a good point that anybody who complained was NEVER going to support us through Patreon—as in never, ever. At the end of the day, there was no real loss."

He did get worried. Things started to decrease. The first month of decrease was followed by the second month of decrease. Those were really hard months as Jonathan was worried he had made a mistake. But with some time under his belt, he realized what had happened. He had maxed out his current audience.

Jonathan talks about "the edge" and keeping your people away from the edge. When you over-deliver value, your audience never even considers canceling their patronage. With these changes, some of his audience might be closer to the edge. Then when their children need braces and bills get tight, you are one of the first things to go. For about eight months, things just flatlined. Then about three months ago, he started seeing increases again.

Why? Because he was getting new listeners. How is Jonathan going to get there? He is doubling down on value.

He was still worried about getting people involved in the show in a timely fashion. What if, instead of doing a long-form show, he did shorter daily shows? To keep it interesting and stay in the same area, he created a game show: *The Trivial Warfare Blitz*. It's a ten-minute version of *Trivial Warfare*. Jonathan explains, "I get three people, and the game is round robin. If you miss two questions, you're out. The last person standing is the winner. Then here is where long-time listeners get sucked in. After recording three episodes of the blitz (producing three winners), I then have one episode pitting the winners against each other. Creating a winner each game means every fourth episode creates a champion. Then when you get three champions, the next match will create the 'Uber Champion.'"

He started another game show called *Four Play*, where one thing always leads to another. For example, Jonathan says, "If I have the words 'Arrow,' 'Bay,' 'Day,' and 'Lantern,' you must figure out they all have the color green in common (Green Arrow, Green Bay, etc.). Four Play is a one-player game, and I can record eight of those shows in about an hour."

Jonathan doesn't fret as much now about people waiting to get on *Trivial Warfare*. The patrons who have pledged at that level are still in line, but now there are other ways to interact with the show and work with Jonathan and *build that relationship*. He also launched *Things That Are BLANK*, which is very similar to the old *$10,000 Pyramid* game show. In the end, you will come away with daily content from Jonathan, and that is moving the needle. His patrons' cups are overflowing.

Relationships—Relationships—Relationships

In speaking with Jonathan, he did mention that one thing that he doesn't spend much time on anymore is looking at his download stats. He is entirely focused on his community. As he keeps moving forward, he keeps meeting more people. The more people he meets, the more doors get opened.

Sporcle is a huge brand in trivia, and through the podcast, Jonathan now has a relationship with a senior VP at Sporcle. He has a relationship with Nick, the CEO of City Trivia (another big trivia company). Like most communities, everyone talks to each other, so a well-connected person in Chicago (Jeremy) told Nick, "You have to listen to Jonathan." For me, this is the definition of "value." When your audience is telling their friends, "You have to listen to this," you are delivering value.

Jonathan did a live show at Trivia Nationals and met all sorts of people who own trivia-related products. He's making friends with all of them. At Dragon Con 2019 Jonathan was asked to do a live show with the McElroys (who are HUGE in podcasting). The live show was in the large ballroom that had an estimated 1,500 "standing-room-only" people watching.

THE ONE THING PATREON DOES THAT OFTEN GETS OVERLOOKED

Comedian Heather McDonald of the *Juicy Scoop Podcast* (heathermcdonald. net) put it this way: "With Patreon, it's not about likes and views, you can really connect with your fans, ignore the haters, and focus on the positive. I'd rather have 300 patrons than three million Instagram followers."

For me, this is the one thing that Patreon (or any tool that assembles your biggest fans) does. It makes it easy to see and connect with your TRUE fans. We scramble around like a chicken with our head cut off, trying to grow our audience. We already have a list of real people who LOVE our show (and more than likely are telling their friends about it). Instead of trying to get cold leads to warm up, why not dump gas on the people who are already on fire for your show?

PATREON ISN'T WORKING FOR ME

I do hear this phrase from time to time. Here are some things you might want to ask yourself.

1. Did you follow the recommended steps?
   a. Did you make a video?
   b. Did you create rewards that are valuable to the audience?
   c. Did you remember to get honest feedback from someone NOT named Mom?
2. How clearly does your Patreon page communicate what you do?
   a. Always try to explain anything to your audience using *their terminology*. Describe things in the way they will understand. Often when we are close to a subject, we drop in a bunch of jargon and leave people confused. While it is helpful to stick with a theme, and make your tiers tie in with your brand, getting too clever can lead to confusion.
3. Does my audience need to take a course to understand how my rewards work or is it easy?
   a. This is where finding someone who is not named Mom comes in handy again. If possible, have them go to your page and talk out loud about the page and then ask them if they know how to become a patron and what they receive.
4. Where did you promote it?
   a. Patreon (much like a sponsor) must be mentioned in every episode, in every post, in social media, and any other place you exist. The phrase "If you build it, they

will come" is a lie. Mention your campaign in your episodes (and explain what they are missing out on, and
how they will benefit). If someone brings up something
you use in the show, BE SURE to mention that the person is a PATRON and mention them BY NAME. If they
have a website, MENTION IT; let your audience see the
benefits of being a patron.

5. How strong is my call to action (CTA)?

    a. We just spoke about the reason people support podcast-
        ers. Are you making it clear what you deliver, how it will
        be delivered, and *how they will benefit*?

PATREON ISN'T THE ONLY OPTION

I've mentioned Patreon here, as they are the biggest ongoing crowdfunding
service. There are others that have popped up, and there are more on the
way. Sites like glow.fm and buymeacoffee.com are designing services aimed
at making it super easy to support podcasters. I'll share more about those in
the tools section. I just wanted to make sure you know there is more to crowdfunding than Patreon.

9

Live Events

It may be hard to comprehend people taking vacation time to come to an event you would organize. More and more podcasters are realizing that they have a certain level of influence and they have built a community that wants to connect on a deeper level. Your impostor syndrome may be kicking in as you hear that voice in your head say, "Wait, they would come here to see ME?" Here are some strategies and tools that you can use to take some of the fear out of creating your own event.

KICKSTARTER CAMPAIGNS

If you're not sure if anyone will show up, there is an easy way to find out. Have them put their money where their mouth is. In 2014 *Podcast Movement* had a goal of raising $11,000 to do an event in Dallas, Texas. They raised $31,854. In 2019 *She Podcasts* had a Facebook group of over 12,000 women who were saying the leaders should start a female-focused podcast event. They started a campaign on Kickstarter with a goal of $25,000 and received $50,547.

With both *Podcast Movement* and *She Podcasts*, they leaned on their community to find speakers and help organize the event. You might be sitting on an event for your genre. If you're not sure, ask around in your community, and if you want to get the ball rolling, you might consider a Kickstarter campaign.

FLYNNCON1

Pat Flynn of *Smart Passive Income* launched his first event in 2019 with Flynncon1. Pat also reached out to his community and interviewed any of his friends who had been involved with organizing events. He met with his planning team and picked a target number for attendees, a hotel, and (this is important) *hired an event organizer* (as did *She Podcasts*). Why? Pat knew that this event reflected his brand. If you're going up Mount Everest, you'd better hire a sherpa. If you are launching your first conference, you'd better hire someone who has organized events before.

Pat started by brainstorming with his team, and they came up with some great ideas. Some of these ideas were close to $200,000 to pull off (and consequently were put into the "maybe next year" pile). By thinking BIG, it starts you thinking of next year, while you transition from what you *want* to what you *need* for THIS year.

If you know Pat, you know he loves his family. Consequently, his event reflected his brand. It was a family-friendly conference with no alcohol. They held the conference in the summer in San Diego, California (Pat's hometown).

LIVE EVENTS ARE BLOWING UP

The number of live, ticketed events based on podcasts has grown by more than 2,000 percent since 2012, according to data from North American ticket vendor Vivid Seats, per Axios.[1]

In a report on the average ticket price for the show:

- *My Favorite Murder*: $117
- *Wait Wait . . . Don't Tell Me!*: $113
- *Pod Save America*: $103
- *Armchair Expert*: $108
- *The Joe Budden Podcast*: $95
- *How Did This Get Made?*: $92
- *The Try Guys*: $84
- *My Brother, My Brother and Me*: $77
- *Last Podcast on the Left*: $72
- *Welcome to Night Vale*: $59
- *Stuff You Should Know*: $58[2]

---

1   Mariel Soto Reyes, "Here's How Live Events Can Help Podcasters Monetize Further," *Business Insider*, July 10, 2019, https://www.businessinsider.com/live -events-offer-podcasters-additional-path-to-monetization-2019-7.

2   "Podcasters Are Packing Listeners in at Live Events," *Inside Radio*, July 9, 2019, http: //www.insideradio.com/podcastnewsdaily/podcasters-are-packing-listeners -in-at-live-events/article_3e4ecc56-a268-11e9-b376-a7077df95607.html.

I investigated *Pod Save America* when they were on tour. Here is the information for two tour stops:

> Byham Theater in Pittsburgh
> Sold out: 1,313 tickets
> Tickets started at $40

If you take 1,313 tickets and multiply it by $40 each, you get $52,520 for one night.

> Radio City Music Hall in New York City
> Two nights
> Capacity: 6,015
> Tickets start at $40[3]

Multiply 6,015 tickets by $40 each, and you get a total ticket sale of $240,600 for one night. If you sell out two nights in a row, the total comes to $481,200.

Now don't go crazy. This is not all profit (you have travel, food, and equipment expenses, and the theater is definitely going to take a chunk); nonetheless, this is another option where you can make money with your podcast.

WHAT IF YOU CAN'T SELL OUT A THEATER?

While it's inspiring to see these large podcasts with huge audiences making tons of money via live events, what if you have a smaller audience, and maybe don't have the engagement to inspire people to travel to see you? This doesn't mean you can't host a live event. There are other options besides Radio City Music Hall.

You could use an online tool such as Zoom (http://bit.ly/zwebinars). For forty dollars per month, you can have an online event that holds up to one hundred people. Their system integrates with PayPal so you can charge for your event. You can interact with your audience, do Q&A, conduct polls (or keep them all on mute). It gives you the ability to get face-to-face with your

---

3   Brittany Frederick, "Pod Tours America Announces 2019 Run," *AXS*, January 17, 2019, https://www.axs.com/pod-tours-america-announces-2019-run-136155.

audience. While you can't shake their hand, you are interacting with them in a live setting.

If you charge twenty dollars a ticket, you would only need two people to buy a ticket to break even. Then you can take the recording and sell the video. We will talk about more tools to help you make money later.

GO TO A PRE-EXISTING EVENT WITH YOUR FANS

This works well for podcasts about sports teams. Nick Seuberling did a show about the Cincinnati Bengals. He organized a bus ride from Cincinnati to Pittsburgh to watch a football game. Nick used a local bus company (rather than a national chain).

I previously mentioned Corey Fineran, who does a show called *Ivy Envy* (ivyenvy.com) about the Chicago Cubs. He will organize meetups at the games. He also has a yearly "Weekend at the Lake" where his audience gets together and has a great weekend of camping and hanging out. He also will organize times to meet at a bar to watch Cubs games together.

John Baker is a famous Cubs catcher, and Corey helps promote and work with the John Baker Day event. According to their website, "The Son Ranto Show and Ivy Envy podcast have helped raise money for charity with Cubs Mental Skills coordinator John Baker to celebrate 'The Night the Backup Catcher Got the Win.'" The event raises money for the Chicago Metropolitan Battered Women's Network. This is just another great example of being where your audience is and building relationships.

THINGS YOU WISH YOU HAD THOUGHT OF AHEAD OF TIME

When going to events, you need to consider if your fans expect to be fed or not (as that would change the ticket price). In the case of Nick, he had a four-hour bus ride. He had purchased some soft drinks and snacks for the trip. When you add food to an event, it can get tricky as you have people who are vegetarian, gluten free, etc. Nick ordered pizza, and luckily the vegetarian attendees could eat a plain cheese pizza. You need to ask the attendees when they sign up if you plan on feeding them.

Other things you might want to check is if anyone has special needs like a wheelchair so you can make sure any locations you will be using have handicap access.

In the case of Nick, he had to put a security deposit on the bus that needed to be paid in full the week before the trip. You might consider running a crowdfunding campaign at Kickstarter to raise the money, and then use the money to book the trip, so there is less of a chance of getting stuck with a bill for an empty bus. Keep in mind not everyone listens to your podcast every week (HOW DARE THEY!). Announcing it months ahead of time gives plenty of time for people to check their schedule and plan.

When it comes to planning, Nick started promoting it six weeks from the event. Looking back, he says he should've started twelve weeks out from the event.

If you are going to do a live show in front of an audience, make sure the venue has a PA system. If the venue doesn't have a PA system (and you realize you will need one), you can get a portable PA system for less than $300 that will fill up most rooms. You can save more money by renting one from your local music store. You can take a portable recorder and plug your microphone into the recorder, and the output of the recorder into the powered speakers. This is where having a mixer can come in handy as it provides the ability to tweak your tone (via bass, middle, treble settings) and avoid feedback. If you're new to live sound, remember to keep the microphones behind the speakers (you want the speakers on the front of the stage with you standing behind them). If you put the microphones in front of the speakers, you risk creating feedback.

Many people are coming to these events to meet YOU, the host. Be sure to have some name tags (and if you have limited seating you might have someone run a registration desk to ensure those who signed up can attend). These can be simple "hello my name is" stickers, or if you want, you can have lanyards made that attendees can keep as a souvenir (which, according to Uncle Google, are around five dollars for a pack of twenty).

In the case of Glenn Hebert's horse cruise, having badges enabled the listeners on the cruise to identify who was part of their group so they could start up conversations.

When you do these live events, it gets you in front of your audience, *builds that relationship,* and creates a great memory. Monetization is possible when you deliver value and leverage the relationship you have with your audience, and events are a great way to build that relationship.

MARK BOLOGNA—*BEYOND BOURBON STREET*

Beyond Bourbon Street is the podcast where Mark Bologna explores the food, music, places, people, and events that make New Orleans unique. The *Beyond Bourbon Street* podcast (beyondbourbonst.com) audience has been nudging Mark to do more local meetups and is volunteering to organize them for him. As of this writing, Mark will be publishing his one hundredth episode and has reached out to local businesses (and has three interested) to do live recordings at their establishments. The businesses Mark chooses will be paying him to do the live recordings at their locations. Businesses want customers in their store, and Mark's audience will come out to support him—and that is worth some compensation.

Recording at a local business is just a variation on the days when the local radio DJ would go to the new grocery store grand opening and do a live remote. This can be another source of revenue. Mark gets four-figure downloads per episode in a hyper-focused market and can guarantee he is going to bring in some customers for the business. These live meetups would be especially well suited for Mark's Q&A episodes. He will do it on a night that might normally be slow for the business to help prove the additional customers are easier to spot, and Mark can take credit for the increase in business.

JOE SAUL-SEHY—*STACKING BENJAMINS*

Joe did a three-city tour for his comedy/financial show *Stacking Benjamins* (www.stackingbenjamins.com). Joe did this tour for one reason, to do something newsworthy, and it worked. He also wanted to meet new fans as well as mix it up and keep the show fresh. When I interviewed him, he said, "I wanted to give people a reason to say 'Stacking Benjamins' over and over and over. I wanted to talk to people who normally wouldn't talk about *Stacking Benjamins* and get them to talk about the show."

If you go to your local paper or TV outlet and say "I have a podcast," they don't care (even if you get inducted into the Podcasters Hall of Fame—ouch). However, if you mention you are on tour, that's newsworthy. In Detroit, Joe was able to get on the news and talk about the event that was coming to town on two local channels. In Orlando, the *Orlando Sentinel* picked up the story. In Kansas City, one TV station picked up the story.

It doesn't have to be that big of an event, depending on the venue. If you are at a local community center, they will put you on the calendar and write about it in the newsletters. There are also local Facebook groups you can search out and let them know you are coming.

Finding the Right Venue

Joe originally looked into punk rock clubs because he thought that would be fun, but club owners wanted nothing to do with a financial podcast (even if it was funny). Joe then contacted comedy clubs, and they were interested in having the tour come to their venue.

As Joe needed venues in multiple cities, he needed someone with a chain of locations. He reached out to the Improv, which is the biggest chain of comedy clubs. Joe realized that his podcast was not going to be a headliner, so he contacted the comedy clubs and found that many of them had nothing on Tuesday nights.

Originally, they wanted to rent Joe the room. This was not ideal and would require money up front. Joe asked, "So when a comedian comes to town do you rent them the room?" and they answered, "No, we sell tickets, and we split the proceeds with them." To this, Joe said, "Let's do that."

When asked what Joe wanted to charge per ticket, Joe asked for the minimum price. This was ten dollars. There was a processing fee of two dollars and fifty cents, so the net income was seven dollars and fifty cents, which was split evenly with Joe. They then asked Joe, "How many people do you think you'll have?" and Joe answered, "A hundred." Then Joe hung up the phone and thought, *How am I going to get a hundred people to these events?*

Joe said, "It's good to push yourself, and at our first event, we had exactly one hundred people." At the second city, there was a tornado, and only forty-five people showed (but they didn't blame Joe). The last room only held one hundred people, and it was standing room only.

Getting the Word Out—Hiring Pros

Joe's goal was to be mentioned in the media. He wanted to get on TV, and to do that he needed to hire some professional PR and advertising companies. He ended up hiring two firms. He mentioned that everything these companies did, you could do yourself. He explained, "We hired people to make press releases, as well as 'splashy stuff' to put on our social media accounts." If you're on a tight budget and understand how to create these things, you might do them yourself.

How did Joe pick his PR firm? He went to those firms that *successfully* pitched things to *Stacking Benjamins*. He went to the people that he best works with, and asked, "What would it cost?" They replied with a gigantic number. Joe replied what his budget was, and *because of their relationship,* they gave him a HUGE discount.

Being a podcaster, Joe reached out and was a guest on twenty-one different podcasts. Joe gets pitched all the time from guests, so he knew how to approach other podcasters. His pitch contained:

- Proof that he listened to the show.
- He pitched an idea that he had not heard lately on their show.
- He mentioned the tour and that he would like to mention it on their show (being transparent), but just needed a mention.

Funding the Tour

How do you fund a tour? For Joe, he said it was OPM (other people's money). He knew up front he needed to cover the PR and advertising, and the traveling costs. He made a slide deck and did some presentations to potential sponsors. The presentation pointed out the cities (Detroit, Orlando, Kansas City) and what would be included in the show. They explained they had hopes of getting on television and how they would mention the sponsor in all appearances. They would also include the sponsor in the show and add their name to any flyers, swag, etc.

Here again, it all boils down to relationships. The CEO for Joe's sponsor had already been on the show. When they said, "We will sponsor it if the CEO can be in the show," Joe knew he was a great guest and said yes immediately. Joe said, "We started with someone we knew. They had already been on the show. We were comfortable with them, and we were pretty sure they would say yes, and they did."

Do a Good Show

Joe knew this had to have some elements that would be different from his regular podcast. Normally all it takes to listen to the show is to put on some headphones. Now, people had to leave home, hire babysitters, etc. Joe had to make it special. He had to deliver value. To start the show, he made a special video with some energetic music that got your blood going. The video showed the tour logo (including the sponsor); it looked professional, and eventually, the video led to a countdown screen and when it got to zero the theme music for the podcast started. It was like a concert opening. It wasn't some people walking on stage and saying, "Check, check, is this on?"

Make Each Show Unique and Spotlight the Locality

For each show, Joe reached out to local musicians to be the opening act. It was a quick fifteen minutes, but this got more people *locally* talking about the *Stacking Benjamins* show.

Do Those Things You Can't Normally Do

To help build up the hype for the show, Joe and crew stayed hidden before it began. However, after they said good night and people applauded, they walked right into the audience and took selfies, and stayed there until everyone had left.

Things Joe Learned from His First Tour

He forgot to ask for copies of the news coverage to put on his website/YouTube.

Joe uses Libsyn to host his podcast files, and he can see the cities where his audience resides. Had he looked at his stats, he would've selected the top three cities where his show is consumed (New York, Los Angeles, and San Francisco). However, Joe didn't do that, and instead picked numbers 14, 17, and 23 (Orlando, Kansas City, and Detroit). By going to where his audience currently is, it might've been easier (or at least less stressful) to sell tickets.

The Result

During the tour, Joe saw his numbers go up 20 percent and long-term 10 percent have stuck around.

GLENN HEBERT'S RADIOTHON HOLIDAY PROMOTION

Glenn Hebert from the Horse Radio Network created a twelve-hour live event. This wasn't a live event where you sold tickets. In fact, it was the opposite. You might walk out with a prize for attending. This wasn't easy. He started planning months in advance when he was face-to-face with the sponsors. He had prewritten posts to go out to everyone's Facebook pages. Sponsors were contractually obligated to mention the event on Facebook (all they had to do was copy and paste the text). This helped get the word out to about a million people via all of the sponsor's Facebook pages, and to audience members.

Glenn mentioned that he had three sponsors fighting over the top spot, and he may entertain the idea of auctioning off the top spot next year (as this is going to be a yearly event).

It included:

- Over twenty hosts
- Thirty scheduled guests including Charlie Daniels, Robin from Disney World, Monty Roberts, and Triple Crown-winning American Pharaoh trainer Bob Baffert
- Crashing the live feed during Bob Baffert; everything else worked all day
- Over 100 listener voice mails with songs, poems, and holiday greetings
- 200 calls during the day (not all got on air)
- Giveaways worth $3,000 and prizes, including a $1,000 grand prize—all donated by the sponsors
- Seventeen sponsors
- Some of the top bloggers in the horse space came on the show and helped promote the event

You might ask, "Wait, how did he get musician Charlie Daniels?" Believe it or not, by using the contact page on his website. Charlie loves Christmas and horses and called in and spent twenty minutes with them over the phone before he went on stage.

People in Glenn's audience knew Bob Baffert, and as Glenn put it, "It's not who you know, it's who knows you."

His audience was writing poems/songs to Christmas music. Glenn mentioned he had a few versions of "The Twelve Days of Christmas" that included his sponsors (which proves engagement to current and future sponsors).

What was the motivation?

- First, as always, Glenn wanted to give back to the fans and make an event to get people to talk about the show. If you want to make the news, you do something newsworthy. If you want word of mouth, you need to do something worth sharing.
- In this case, Glenn knew that he had some sponsors who wouldn't currently sponsor week to week or month to month, but they might do a "one off" sponsorship of an event.
- His normal podcast is ninety minutes long. Now he had twelve hours of content to put advertising into.
- He did it on Cyber Monday, as everyone had their wallets out and were in a buying mood (which his sponsors loved).

Glenn has continued to do this every year, and last year gave away about $5,000 in prizes. This really spurs the number one thing that grows your audience—word of mouth—while spurring future advertisers.

GLENN HEBERT: HORSE LOVERS' CRUISE

Glenn put it this way: "We went on vacation with our super listeners who quickly became friends." One of Glenn's listeners (Rhonda) did all the work. She had been on a bunch of cruises. She had also listened to *all* 6,700 episodes of the Horse Radio Network. She was great and answered a ton of questions for people. Glenn sold so many tickets, he was given some free tickets and gave one to Rhonda for all the work she did.

Every night at dinner, Glenn made everyone switch spots, so the group of forty people got to know each other. They already had something in common to talk about (Glenn's show), and this built a bridge so that the listeners could create their relationships with one another and build the bond of community.

Glenn recounts, "We had lanyards made that had our logo so everyone could tell who our group was. We had the sponsor make up gift bags, and we gave away some close to $1,500 worth of prizes. We didn't want this to be formal. There were no presentations, etc. We did one game show where everyone won something, and we ate together. We just wanted to have fun and build our community. It was a blast, and we are already booking next year."

LOCAL PODCAST EVENTS

There are two types of podcast events. Some focus on helping people plan, launch, grow, and monetize their show. This typically includes a vendor showcase with microphones, media hosts, and more.

The second type of podcast event is more of a podcast spotlight. Think of it like music events where multiple bands come together, and music lovers listen to all the bands. The difference is instead of bands, you listen to a podcaster perform their content live.

For example, if you lived in Chicago, you might want to get involved with the Chicago Podcast Festival (chicagopodcastfestival.org). This is organized by the Chicago Improv Festival. There is also an LA Podfest and others.

But, Dave, how does this make money? Okay, you got me. In this case, you wouldn't get paid, but you would get in front of podcast listeners and some cases YOUR listeners, and that is priceless.

10

Opportunities

Many opportunities come into view when you start a podcast. These opportunities can be paid, and many lead to other opportunities that can lead to other opportunities. Here is an example.

Because of my podcast, I've been able to speak at Podcast Movement every year. One year at Podcast Movement I happened to be talking to Mike Morrison (membershipacademy.com), who also knows Pat Flynn (smartpassiveincome.com), whom I also know. Michael Stelzner (socialmediaexaminer.com) walked up, and we started talking podcasting. This led to me talking at Social Media Marketing World. One opportunity led to me grow my network, which led to more opportunities, which led to more. All of these allowed me to grow my audience and my customer base (not to mention they look good on a speaking résumé).

I was asked to speak at an event for independent publishers in San Francisco. The organizer had found my podcast via Google (yet another reason you need a website). The local radio station saw I was coming to town and knew podcasting is a super-hot topic. I went on the station and gave a great interview. I had done some research about the DJ and station beforehand. This led to the DJ researching me, and she saw that *Profit from Your Podcast* (you know—the book you're reading) was coming out in a few months and scheduled a return interview to talk about the book.

SPEAKING GIGS

Speaking gigs (especially paying speaking gigs) are something that most podcasters yearn to obtain. After all, you achieve your goals of getting in front of your target audience as well as getting paid. Here are some things to consider.

You need a demo reel—some video of you speaking in front of an audience. Talking into a webcam is not you talking in front of an audience. Likewise, a webinar (while it has an audience) is not you in front of a group of people onstage. You may want to consider volunteering to speak for free at an event. If you don't have a fancy camera, an iPhone or most other smartphones take amazing video. However, the one thing that will reduce the quality of the video quickly is the audio. You can use the Zoom H1 recorder (which is about the size of a Snickers bar) and clip on a lavalier microphone and then later add the audio from your recording into the video. When you use the video from the iPhone recording, you pick up all the room noise. If possible, work with the sound crew to get a recording off their soundboard if they're using one.

Then put yourself in the shoes of the person who selects the speakers. The first thing they are going to do when they look at your video is to look at the bottom right hand corner and check the length of the video. Think of this as a movie trailer. A movie trailer's job is to get you excited to see the movie. You want your speaker reel to do the same thing. But movie trailers are quick, and your speaker reel should follow that example. You want it to be three minutes or less.

Think of your greatest hits. If you use humor, use your best jokes that make sense even if you don't get the setup. If you have a section that makes people think, include that. You can edit the video to be multiple segments spliced together with some transitions, or you might find the best two minutes of a talk you have and use that segment.

At the end of the demo reel be sure to include your contact information, as the demo reel may get separated from your original submission and you don't want someone watching to say, "Hey that person is really good—who is that and where can we find them again?" If you want to go the extra mile record a quick, personalized intro such as, "Hey, this is Dave Jackson, and I want to thank you for watching my demo reel. I appreciated the chance to be considered for (the opportunity name)." Keep this *brief* if you use this strategy. Remember, the booking person wants to see you speak in front of a live audience.

The bottom line is most people who are looking for speakers want to see and hear them speak.

Speaking Is a Lot Like Podcasting

If you go super niche on your speaking subjects, you may have fewer people who need to hear your talk. You want to figure out the problem you solve, and who needs to hear it. In podcasting, the more niche you go, the stronger the connection you have with the audience (but the lower the number of downloads). With speaking it is different; if you go too niche, then there won't be enough opportunities to speak.

In podcasting, you start with knowing your audience. In speaking it's about knowing your conference/event. Look for any buzzwords in their description of the event and try to work those into the description of your session, if they fit.

See what pains that audience is suffering from and come up with a talk that explains how to solve their pain.

Own Your Opinion and Make It Good

If your answer to "What do you speak about?" is "everything," you need to go back to the drawing board. I talk about podcasting. Could I talk about social media? I might be able to pull something together. Could I talk about SEO? Again, I can throw some topics together. If you give people a list of nine different topics, you may inspire people to think you are a jack of all trades (and a master of none) when they want an *expert* on this one thing. I tend to stay in my lane, acknowledge my strengths, and talk about podcasting.

Should I Speak for Free?

This is a question that is going to be different for each person reading this book. If you are a busy parent with kids and a spouse at home, flying hours away and missing days away from your family is more of a burden than the person who has no family responsibilities. I currently have no spouse, no kids, no pets. I can stay out way past when the streetlights are on, and nobody cares.

Someone who has family responsibilities may be more willing to talk for free if they know the creator of the event (again with the relationships) and the event is local. If it's a new event that they've never heard of, and it requires days away from their family, they may choose to pass on this opportunity.

The other thing to consider is your audience. I once spoke at a "Wordcamp," which is an event for people using WordPress. I figured the conference would have a lot of bloggers there, and some of them might want to repurpose their content as a podcast. The event was about fifteen minutes from my house. I went and attended the night before when they had a "mixer" for the speakers to get acquainted with one another. It was here that I noticed that most of the speakers were involved more with the back end of WordPress (coding, developing) than the front end as a content creator.

When it came time to do my presentation (that I had worked hard on—more on that in a minute), I spoke in front of five people (including the staff member who was there to alert me when I had five minutes left). Do some research if you can and see if you can find someone in your community who has attended the event in the past. Was this a failure? It may appear this way, but if nothing else, it was more practice at public speaking. The challenge, in this case, was keeping my excitement when talking to a room that would hold about fifty people and had only five. I always try to find a way to grow or learn something.

One question you want to ask is if you can guarantee that you will be on during one of the "regular" days of the event. I once was asked MONTHS in advance to speak at an event. I was thrilled to be asked, and the audience seemed like a good fit. To make a very long story short, I ended up speaking on what I call a "warm-up" day (the day before the conference where they often put in workshops). These days before the actual event often pull in a fraction of the attendees.

Also, make sure you get a recording of the presentation for you to use (remember that demo reel). This is especially true if you are doing this for free. If nothing else, you should get a copy of your presentation for free.

I recently spoke at an event for financial influencers. I was not paid to speak. However, this audience had a lot going for it:

- Fincon was in its ninth year of the event (and it had thousands of people attending).
- The audience had a budget (it was financial bloggers, etc.).
- It had a good word of mouth, and I heard that this was a good event to attend.

I was happy to speak for free, and it paid off.

The Best Marketing Tool Is a Great Talk

One thing I do before every one of my talks is greeting people as they come in. If they are there first, I'll ask them what they expect to get out of the talk and start doing an impromptu poll.

Why? What is the one thing I repeat over and over in this book? *Know your audience.* When I spoke at the National Speakers Association (NSA), right before I started the official talk, I asked for a raise of hands to see who already had a podcast and who was looking to start one. This allowed me to see if I needed to slow down or speed up in any areas where there wasn't much interest.

I was very pleased with my talk at the NSA. At the end of the presentation, I had a good number of people who personally approached me about how much they got out of the session. If this happens to you, don't forget to think ahead, and ask if they don't mind repeating what they just said into your phone while you record it (so you can put this testimonial on your "speaker page"). I got a handful of new subscribers to my podcast (more on how I track that later), and if you've set up a landing page for anyone who wants your slides, you can grow your email list as well. I had great conversations with quite a few people before and after my talk (who turned into clients), making it a pretty lucrative presentation.

Keep Yourself in Check

If this is your first time speaking at a conference, you may find yourself in a situation where the organizer isn't very organized. There may not be many attendees. You may not be able to find out where your room is located. You have a live band setting up behind you (true story), or the audio/video systems are awful, etc. Do not let the disorganization alter your attitude toward the attendees. I've made some great contacts and partnerships at events that were a hot mess from head to toe.

Always remember your voice. At many events, large companies will sponsor a large "networking party" for the event. For whatever reason, these companies (often against the advice of the event organizer) will hire a live band or DJ and turn the networking party into what I affectionately refer to as "ear-bleeding madness." Loud events lead to you to shouting at people. If this is the night before your presentation, do the smart thing and call it a night, or find another (quieter) place to meet people.

Bits and Pieces to Check When Speaking

To summarize, the things to keep an eye on include:

- Are they paying for travel?
- Are they paying for the hotel if you need one?
- Are they paying for food?

- Is your talk part of the conference, or is it part of a "pre-conference" presentation?
- Is this a breakout session or a keynote?
- Do you get a ticket to the event?
- Do you get access to any recordings (especially yours)?
- If you're getting paid, when will you be paid (before or after the talk)?

How Much Should I Charge?

How much you should charge is one of those questions that ends with everyone's favorite answer, "It depends." It depends on your niche (the fewer people who can talk about your subject, the more you can charge). You can use a tool kit by Grant Baldwin to get a better idea of pricing; use his speaker fee calculator at thespeakerlab.com/toolkit.

Tips for Speaking

When the event organizer says "No selling from the stage," they mean it. You might want to double-check to make sure giving away your slides in return for their email is okay. One thing to keep in mind is people who run events frequently attend other events. I was at one event when a presenter went into a *hard* pitch (the typical "Normally $7,999, but just this weekend $3,997"). They stood out like a sore thumb, as everyone else had followed the rules of no selling from the stage. What this person didn't realize was the organizer of a large event was in the corner watching the whole thing. Not only did this person not get asked back to the original event, but it also ruined their chances of speaking at the larger event.

I was the head of the podcasting track for the (now-defunct) New Media Expo. Selecting speakers is a hard job. Some of these people you will know, which can make the situation awkward. I was amazed at how many people barely put any information into their proposal. I had stated what we were looking for and asked for clear takeaways for their sessions. Here are some of the things that amazed me:

- People didn't list any takeaways (I'm guessing they copied and pasted their presentation from some document they had lying around and didn't want to be bothered to edit it). You should have crystal-clear learning objectives. For example:

At the end of my presentation, the audience will be able to
_____.

- They would fail to include their website address. In case I didn't know the potential speaker and I wanted to learn more about them, there was a field for a website, and they left it blank.

- Once approved, they needed to send a headshot and a bio. A headshot and bio isn't asking a lot, but for some people, it was like pulling teeth. Don't be a pain in the ass.

- Don't take things personally or throw a tantrum. Some speakers let their ego get in the way. They want to get paid to speak. If the gig you are trying to get doesn't pay, then politely decline. If you need to ask the question, "Do you know who I am?" then whoever wrote your bio needs to be fired. Also, keep in mind that in some years, events just want new faces. Don't take it personally if you aren't asked. Yes, it sucks to go on before or after lunch. Don't forget that there are *tons* of people who would *die* to take your place on the stage.

- In some cases, events don't have the budget to pay, or pay much. Keep in mind that this is an event around your niche. If you throw a tantrum, there is a good chance the booking agent knows other people in your niche (or in some cases books multiple events). Always be polite. Thank them for the opportunity and inform them you need to decline. If you want to go the extra mile, suggest a good speaker who might be willing to do the gig for what they are offering.

- Always start and end on time. If you end your session with Q&A, keep an eye on the clock. Don't be "that guy/girl" who won't get off the stage. Otherwise, when the next speaker needs to configure their presentation, you've made their life stressful. You may be the reason the next session starts late, and in general, people will not want to work with you. I practice my presentations over and over (twenty to fifty times) before I do them. I time each practice run as I often will be inspired to tweak a slide or add a point the more I do it. I purposely plan my presentation to end ten minutes early. Why? Because I *know* I will "call an audible" during the presentation and improvise some points that come to my head while presenting. This way I still end on time.

- Pay attention to details. There will be emails from the organizer as the event gets closer. Be sure to read all those emails. When it comes to events, nobody likes surprises.

- Make sure you have everything you need to successfully put on your presentation. If you're going to be speaking, make sure your laptop has all the cables to connect to just about any projector. If you only have VGA out of your laptop, you better buy a VGA to HDMI converter (as well as an HDMI to VGA converter). I often bring a portable speaker with me in case there is no audio.

- Be careful about including audio/video in your presentation. I typically try to avoid audio and video in my presentations. Why? Because I'm often presenting at locations that have either poor or no Internet access at all. Consequently, if I include video, I download the video to my computer, so I'm not streaming it over the Internet. I once did a presentation at a business, and my presentation had a YouTube video in it. The location I was presenting at blocked YouTube. That goes for audio as well. I save my slide deck, audio, and video all into a single folder. Then everything is running locally (and not over the Internet). Typically, I avoid using audio/video unless it is necessary to make a point.

- If the event requires you to email your presentation to them ahead of time, stick to traditional fonts in your presentation. If you've used some "special" font, and it's not on the machine they are using, the computer will substitute a different font, and this often does not end well.

- If you have a panel, make sure the team practices. Do not wait until the last minute to figure out who is saying what. Panels can be a one-way ticket to never being asked back. Organizers often use panel presentations to see if you can follow the rules and not cause headaches. I have heard of speakers who are new in their niche approaching events and volunteering to be a moderator if they put together a panel. Why? Because some people (again due to ego) don't want to be on a panel. When you volunteer, you are already showing that you are easygoing. Then next year (after you've *built that relationship*), you can submit for your breakout session.

- If there is some survey for the audience at the event, remind the audience to review your session.

OTHER OPPORTUNITIES

I do a segment of my show called "Because of My Podcast" where members of my audience share opportunities that have come their way (and wouldn't have happened otherwise) because of their podcast. These include:

Building Your Network

If you went to someone and said, "Hey, you don't know me, Mr. CEO, but can I have thirty minutes of your time?" you would receive a short two-letter answer: "No." One of the biggest advantages of podcasting is getting to speak to people with whom you have *no business taking up their time*. When I first started my podcast for musicians, I got to talk to my idols. You can't put a price on that.

Travel

In some cases, organizations will pay to have you come to an event (more on that in a bit). I mentioned Chris Christensen at the beginning of the book. If you look at his website amateurtraveler.com, you will see all the places he has been.

Glenn Hebert (when he's not talking about horses) is a cohost with Jaime Legagneur on the *Finding Florida* podcast. Jaime reached out to the local tourism board right after episode three. She got press passes for a tourism event in Florida. They paid for Glenn and Jaime to come to the event, as well as hotel and food for three days.

The tourism board said that Glenn and Jaime were the first podcasters to ask to come to the conference and *they were thrilled* that they *finally* had a podcaster at the conference. Now Glenn and Jaime have gone on many adventures, and the tourism bureaus for the locations they are visiting pay for everything (including VIP passes to EVERYTHING). The local people created an itinerary and had it all planned out (including guests). The show has gone from costing the price of travel to doing it for free. Glenn feels in the future they will be paid to visit locations, as they are giving the locations so much exposure. A side note: not one person asked how many downloads their podcast was getting.

In true Glenn fashion, he and Jaime have grown their show into a network all about Florida (floridapodcastnetwork.com/).

Books/Print/Media

Emily Prokop of *The Story Behind* (thestorybehindpodcast.com) podcast was approached by a publisher to turn her podcast episodes into a book.

Jeremy Dennis of the *Transmissions Podcast* (transmissionspodcast.com) had his face on a custom cover of a comic book.

Danielle Daily from the *Suddenly Single* podcast (suddenlysingleshow.com) has been featured on the cover of a magazine and interviewed.

Over the years I've had clients get press passes, free trips, free hotels, interviews with people they have no business interviewing (but they got to because of their podcasts). Arnie Chapman is known as the Football History Dude (thefootballhistorydude.com). When I interviewed him, he explained how he got a press pass during the Hall of Fame week for the NFL in Canton, Ohio. He said it was amazing to be in a room filled with Hall of Fame football players. While the new inductees got most of the attention, Arnie was more interested in some of the "older" players and got a ton of interviews and connections.

When you develop a community of people who rely on and trust your opinion, you are an "influencer," and companies know that if they can get you to say "I like this product," your audience is likely to purchase it.

Gary Leland gets tickets to the Women's College World Series (for fast-pitch softball) because he has the *Fast Pitch Softball* network (fastpitchradio.com). Because of all his work in the community, there was an official "Gary Leland Day."

I run a local Northeast Ohio Podcasters meetup (neohiopodcasters.com). I never get more than ten people showing up. One of the attendees (who works in local TV) was Matt Rafferty from *The Author Inside You* podcast (theauthorinsideyou.com). My podcast got the attention of Matt. Matt works at a local television station. Through our *relationship* it led to an opportunity to go on a TV show called *Golden Opportunities* and explain podcasting to people over fifty. Yes, it's not Jimmy Fallon, but it looks good on my website.

Tory Heinritz and his cohost Aaron Peterson of *The Blacklist Exposed* (theblacklistexposed.com) have done everything you would want to do with a television podcast. They've interviewed all the actors, writers, and producers of the show *The Blacklist*, and hosted a panel with the producer at Comic Con. They were flown out to California to do interview the producers for the "Behind the Blacklist" promotions, which are often included in the DVD (and aired on TV in the UK). In one episode a character stays at the "Heinritz Institute." *The Blacklist* producers and writers are smart to weave in inside "jokes" and fan the theories that they are aware of because they listen to *The Blacklist Exposed*.

I could go on with "Because of My Podcast" stories for hours. Just keep in mind that while these activities may not always put money in your pocket, they often put you in touch with people and opportunities that might put money in your pocket in the future.

11

Free Stuff

When I receive a piece of equipment for my show, the grocery store won't take it; I can't use a microphone as a form of payment. However, not having to shell out money to buy a piece of equipment you were going to review, or an event ticket, etc., does keep money in your pocket. It also positions you as an influencer. When Rode launched their new RØDECaster Pro production studio (a combination of mixer and recorder all in one), I knew it was going to be a big hit in the podcasting space. I could see where this would fit a large chunk of my audience. Here is how I went about owning this great product without paying for it.

First, I didn't contact the sales department. Their job is to try to sell me their products. I went to the marketing department. Why? Because the job of the marketing department is to get the word out about this product.

When I explain how good I would be at things like:

- Promoting their product on my podcast
- Promoting it in my newsletter
- Doing a video review for YouTube

. . . I often find the answer to "Can I have a review unit?" is "Yes."

You can also be where some manufacturers aren't. There was a manufacturer who wasn't going to be at a very large event for podcasters. I love their gear. I contacted the marketing department and asked for some things to demo and explained that I would be walking around this event using their product. By having me walk around with their product, it gets their product in front of their target audience, positions me as an influencer, and leads to more sales of their product. It is a win-win.

I've heard of podcasters who contact companies to sponsor trips to events. The trade is they typically walk around wearing the company's swag, potentially using their product, and in return, the company gets lots of mentions on the podcast when they talk about the event.

Getting back to my RØDECaster Pro story: Rode let me know they would be in contact when the product was available. I kept my eyes peeled for reviews on YouTube, and the minute I saw the first one, I reached back out to my marketing contact and pointed out that it sure looked like they were available. I pointed out that my audience is made up of podcasters (again, connecting the dots to make it easy for them). I just kept explaining how they would benefit.

Not only did I get to demo a unit, but they also sent me a special version of the equipment that came in a special travel case with two Rode microphones, cables, and a T-shirt. I never assumed I could keep it, but when I offered to send it back, I was told I could keep it.

For the publicity I did (Twitter, Facebook, YouTube), I copied the marketing team so they could see I was a man of my word. Later in the year, they did a big giveaway. They approached me (*because of our relationship*) to help promote it and asked if I wanted to provide a prize in the giveaway. I gave away a one-year membership to the School of Podcasting. This was mentioned in every promotion they sent out about the giveaway.

Here again, knowing your target audience, and giving them what they wanted, led to a great relationship.

While we are talking about free stuff, you will see the "Law of Reciprocity" in full effect when you go to events with your audience. At Podcast Movement 2018 in Philadelphia, I was speaking, and I was honored to be inducted into the Academy of Podcasters Hall of Fame (sorry for the humble brag). I don't believe I paid for a meal the entire time I was there. My audience was excited about the induction, and they wanted to celebrate. Consequently, I'd go to lunch with people and the next thing I knew, we were leaving and my bill had been paid. I never count on this, but it's always very humbling when it happens. I always want to buy their meal as a way of saying thank you for listening.

12

Should I Start a Podcast Network?

You might be wondering if starting a podcast network is a way to make money with your podcast. It seems to make sense. If you have a small show and you want to get a sponsor, they may not sponsor a smaller show. However, if you pull your numbers together, a sponsor might sponsor multiple shows around the same subject.

When I asked a few podcast network organizers about starting a network, they all said variations of "don't." If you are going to do it, run it as a business from day one. As Christopher Brian Jones from Trek.fm put it, "If you think podcasting is hard and time-consuming, try doing it with sixteen different shows. It's really, really hard work."

When you start a podcast, you need to be able to state your why. When starting a network, this even more important. If the answer is "It sounds fun," don't do it.

TWO TYPES OF NETWORKS

One type of podcast network is set up as a business where you pull your resources together to get sponsors. The other type of podcast network is primarily focused on cross-promotion across shows.

As we are focusing on monetization, we somewhat want both. We want shows that have a common theme (horses, hiking, dancing, microbrews) as those are easier to monetize. We also want them to cross-promote as the more promotion you receive, the bigger the potential audience.

From the beginning, you need to define what the purpose of the network is and what it will do for anyone involved. You also need to create criteria for who you will add to the network, the process of adding someone to a network, and the process and criteria for removing someone from your network.

Create a contract between the network and the hosts. This defines what is expected, how people get paid, what will get people fired, and *every other situation you can think of that may happen.* By having these (at times) awkward conversations, you avoid awkward conversations in the future. When people know what will happen if they want to leave, they can plan accordingly, and expectations are set, and you can go through that situation without sacrificing the personal relationship because the business relationship didn't work.

Paying hosts a percentage of the advertisement (in some cases, based on downloads) is a headache you may want to avoid. While this seems fair, it can be a mathematical nightmare. Let's say you have three shows on your network, and the current number of downloads breaks down to:

- Show A: 30%
- Show B: 10%
- Show C: 60%

Let's say you earn $100 in sponsorship for the network. Show A would earn $30. Show B would earn $10. Show C would earn $60.

Breaking it down more:

- Show A creates 4 episodes in a month. This results in $7.50 an episode.
- Show B creates 4 episodes in a month. This results in $2.50 an episode.
- Show C does 20 episodes in a month. This results in $3.00 an episode.

Without the right maturity, Show C may not understand how they bring in most of the downloads, but Show A is making more money per episode (even though their total downloads double the overall amount). Show C might have an average number of downloads per episode that is fewer than the other shows, but as they do more episodes a month, they have more total downloads. Think things through. Try to ponder every scenario. Why? In the immortal words of Cyndi Lauper, "Money Changes Everything."

Also, keep in mind that often the total number of downloads in a month are NOT episodes created during the current month. For example, in July 2019, 60 percent of the downloads for the School of Podcasting were NOT released in July 2019 (it was my audience downloading my older episodes).

Some networks pay a "finder's fee" for bringing in their own sponsor. The more shows you add, the more paperwork it creates.

I bring up these scenarios to show that it can create a mathematical nightmare. When you tie that nightmare into paying people, it can get ugly fast.

The bottom line is *you need to think this through*. It is a lot of extra work.

SHOULD I JOIN A PODCAST NETWORK?

Okay. You thought it through and after seeing all the extra work you've decided not to create your own podcast network. However, you've been approached to join an already existing podcast network. Here again, this seems like a good idea as it might bring more opportunities. Here are some things to consider:

- To join, do you need to switch your media host? If the answer is yes, do not do this until you know what it takes to leave this network, and if they offer a "redirect" that enables you to take your audience with you. Switching your podcast feed is major surgery (and can lead to you losing your entire audience if not done properly).
- Find someone on the network and ask them what the effect of being on the network has done for their download numbers. What is the benefit of being on the network? If they answer "cross-promotion," ask them if their audience saw visible growth after joining the network. Just because there is cross-promotion does not mean it leads to more listeners.
- Ask the network what the details are if you get your own sponsor.
- Is part of the "bonus" or "advantage" of being on the network a banner ad rotated on the website? (Because that's not much of a bonus.)

13

How Much Money Do You Want to Make?

You read about escaping the nine-to-five cubicle and getting the life of your dreams. Let's work things backward and come up with the dollar amount you want to make per year and see what you need to charge for your products and services.

WHAT YOU NEED TO DO TO BRING HOME $60,000

There are tools online you can use to see how much money you need to have a certain take-home pay after taxes. I live in Ohio, and using the Salary Calculator (us.thesalarycalculator.co.uk/salary.php), I see that if I want to have a take-home pay of $60,000 a year, I need to make an annual salary of $75,425.73 However, if you're married with children, you might be paying for health insurance via an organization like COSE (Council of Smaller Enterprises, an Ohio organization that helps small businesses). That insurance can be around $1,700 a month, or $20,400 a year), which would mean you would need to have $95,825.73 in gross revenue to take home $60,000.

Now, if we break that down: $95,825.73 divided by 52 is $1,842.80 per week. Assuming you are working forty hours a week ($1,842.80 divided by 40), that is $46.07 per hour. There are some things to keep in mind. This means, if you're doing consulting, your calendar is booked from morning to night. This also means you're never taking a vacation.

Wait, you want two weeks of paid vacation? Then you need to make $95,825.73 per year ($95,825.73 divided by 50 weeks = $1,916.51 per week). This then means your rate is $47.91 per hour, working forty hours per week, for fifty weeks of the year.

Therefore, some people charge what appears to be inflated pricing for their services. Keep in mind, when they are searching for leads and new customers, they are not making money. This means they need to raise their hourly fee. That raise will pay for those times when they are doing things—like paperwork, taxes, and marketing—that don't directly make money. But you need to run your business (and that is why so many entrepreneurs end up working way more than forty hours a week, as they didn't budget in the amount of time it takes to run the business).

14

One Last Way Podcasters Generate Income

When I speak with podcasters at events, in my communities, there is a common skill that they use to generate income. That skill is podcast consulting/editing. Your audience knows, likes, and trusts you and thinks podcasting is cool. Consequently, they may ask you how you got into podcasting as they are thinking of starting a podcast of their own.

THEY WANT TO LEARN PODCASTING FROM YOU

Mark Bologna from *Beyond Bourbon Street* (beyondbourbonst.com) mentioned how he would send potential podcasters to the School of Podcasting or other podcast consultants. When he spoke to the person who started a podcast, they said they were happy to be podcasting, but had hoped to give some money to Mark. They wanted to learn from Mark. As Mark listened to his audience, he decided to put the time and effort into creating a course, and in fact already helps local businesses launch their podcasts.

Glenn Hebert, who runs the Horse Radio Network (horseradionetwork.com), was approached by magazines and other people in the horse community who wanted to start a podcast. Glenn helped them launch their podcast, outsource their editing, and get them up and running on his network. As more people approached Glenn, he set up his own production team. If he outsources the editing, etc., he gets a piece of the action.

As someone who has been consulting people for over fifteen years, let me tell you that being a podcast consultant is not as easy as putting your shingle out there and watching the money fall from heaven. You answer a lot of questions for free before you get someone to hire you.

You might not be one of those people who wants to dive into being a teacher/consultant. I play the guitar and have since I was twelve years old (I can hold my own). My background is in teaching, but for some reason, I don't enjoy teaching others how to play the guitar. You may be in the same boat. You like podcasting, but you don't want to teach it. Don't forget I have an affiliate program for the School of Podcasting.

15

So You Want to Quit Your Day Job?

Many people dream of being an entrepreneur and launching their businesses and one day leaving their cubicles for the life they've only dreamed about. Here are some of the things I've noticed about people doing this full-time.

MULTIPLE STREAMS OF INCOME

In interviewing different podcasters, I noticed that most of them have multiple streams of income. As I stated before, it's hard to make it *just using sponsors*. It's also hard to make it with just a membership site, etc. Here are some examples:

Jim Harold, *Paranormal Podcast* (jimharold.com)

Jim has been podcasting since 2005. He has numerous books on paranormal topics. He is always interacting with his audience. His one podcast, *Jim Harold's Campfire*, is based on his audience sending in their spooky stories. When you work as hard as Jim and stay consistent, you end up with five-figure downloads per episode. When I interviewed Jim he said, "It took seven years to go full-time. Now, there are people probably better, smarter, and faster than me, and they could ramp up a lot faster than that. But let's say they are three times faster and it takes them two and a half years. It absolutely can be done, and I encourage them to try it. But don't think you're going to quit your job tomorrow. If you do, I hope you have a nice savings account.

"Here is the model I used," Jim said. "I ramped up my podcast on the side while I worked a full-time job. I have a wife and two kids. I started looking at what I was making with podcasting and what I was making at my job. It wasn't equal, but my podcasting income was approaching it. My wife works part-time, and I eventually made the jump."

If you're doing this as a business, even though you could be passionate and interested in the subject, which I am, you must think of it *as a business*. You need *multiple* streams of income. When Jim told me what he pays for health insurance, I about fell out of my chair. These are the expenses you want to investigate before "escaping your cubicle."

Jim has a "plus club" that he manages via Libsyn using their "MyLibsyn" program (libsyn.com/mylibsyn/) program, where he can automatically put some of his episodes behind a paywall. When Jim broke down his income, his revenue streams were

1. Membership/plus club
2. Ad sales
3. Book sales

Jim's advice on choosing advertisers: "I'm a big proponent of not promoting anything you wouldn't personally use. You might win in the short term, but in the long term, you lose because people will try and hate it, or have a bad experience. That can reflect badly on you."

Lessons Learned: "I used to have multiple systems put together to create my 'plus club,' and if one of those systems broke down, I didn't get paid. While I pay a slightly higher fee to use Libsyn to handle my Plus Club, the peace of mind and time I got back was well worth it."

Glenn Hebert, Horse Radio Network (horseradionetwork.com)

When I spoke with Glenn Hebert he mentioned that even though most of his income is from sponsors (about 60 percent), he does have multiple streams of income, including 30 percent from podcast production work, and about 10 percent from listener support (Patreon.com).

Daniel J. Lewis, *The Audacity to Podcast* (theaudacitytopodcast.com)

When I spoke with Daniel, his income looked like this:

- 35% affiliate income
- 6% percent digital products/courses
- 13% software as a service
- 19% membership
- 14% advertising

- 3% percent from donations

Daniel explains that his diversity of income helps keep the stress leverage manageable. When one area of income may have a slight dip, another area might have a surge.

PODCASTING FOR A LIVING

Tim Paige is an entrepreneur who is a voice-over guy. Check out Tim at thevoiceoftimpaige.com or www.makemyintro.com. He is doing the job he loves: working as a voice-over artist. (If you've ever heard an advertisement for Jimmy Kimmel's show on ABC, you've probably heard Tim.) He was working at a job that he liked, but always thought about doing voice-over full-time. He posted on Facebook about how to quit your day job. Here are some tips from Tim:

> Don't quit your day job until it costs you more than you're making in your full-time job not to leave. When the opportunities you must turn down are worth more financially than your full-time job is making you—it's time to quit your day job.
>
> Don't do it because "with the added hours, I have so much more potential." That's dangerous. Instead, do it because you literally must turn down the work.

Tim also points out that he has an incredibly supportive and wonderful wife who supports Tim chasing his dreams.

1. Get Out of Debt

Tim says he had quite a bit of debt, and it took years and years to work his way out of it. At one point he was working three jobs. He had side hustles and freelanced and did whatever it took. For a time, he says he didn't go out or buy anything new.

Being out of debt made it so much less stressful to take the leap. He didn't have to worry about a TON of bills every month. He stated, "Even on a really bad month, we're okay because we don't have huge debt payments going out."

2. Reinvest

For the first three years, Tim reinvested every single penny he made doing voice-over back into the business. This is hard for people to do because they have bills, they want to enjoy the fruits of their labor, and putting that income back into your business is tough.

Tim says that by reinvesting money into his business, it accelerated his career. The reinvesting allowed him to make the jump to full-time quicker.

What kind of reinvesting did Tim do?

He bought coaching. He says, "I bought coaching before I even knew what voice-over really was (it helped me avoid the steep learning curve that's at the beginning of any voice actor's career). I don't know what others have spent on coaching and training, but any time I've shared the number with someone, they've been blown away. But I was going all in, and so far, it has paid off."

Tim would eventually upgrade his gear. Then again later, he bought a hanging vocal booth as he was in an apartment at the time. Then later, when he bought a house, he built a custom booth.

Reinvesting meant Tim's first agent is one of the biggest in the world.

Reinvesting meant money spent on a website, branding, education, events, and courses.

Does Tim still invest every dollar? He says, "Today I don't reinvest every dollar I make back into the business. But I do reinvest a good portion of it because I'm not resting on my laurels. I want to get better. I have a long way to go, and I'm playing the long game here."

3. Be Open to Opportunity

Tim did voice-over for some industries that typically don't ever use voice-over. He was able to take those clients who've hired him and turn them into some of the most lucrative accounts. This wouldn't have happened if Tim wasn't open to it. According to Tim, "My eyes are always scanning for what's next. How can I provide value? How I can fit into the marketplace?"

It wasn't all smooth for Tim, though. He says, "I've made the mistake of doing the opposite during my short voice-over career. I got too myopic. I focused on the area of voice-over I most wanted to work on and closed off the other areas. This really hurt my business, and it took me a while to get back on track.

"I've found that being open to interesting opportunities has afforded me the peace of mind to be in the moment when those dream opportunities come up. The 'less fun' stuff pays the bills, and the dream stuff lights me up inside."

4. Get Your Mind Right

Attitude is a subject where Tim says he still faces struggles.

Tim noticed that the times his business is doing the worst usually occur when his mind isn't right (too desperate, needy, envious). He might've been too focused on what's not working. Tim says, "I'd be too focused on what I don't have, instead of what I have. When I'm looking at peers, *friends* even, and thinking, *I wish I had that. I didn't get that audition; why not? I guess I'm not in the same league as them.*"

Tim says that "When I clear my mind, focus on what I'm grateful for, and just do my thing, then things seem to come together. I can be in the moment during auditions. I can focus on delivering on the script, instead of trying to book a job. It's not so much about *me* anymore as it is about delivering the value my potential clients and my clients need.

"With a crappy mind-set, *everything* is harder. And you can't wait for things to get better before you fix your mind-set. The mind-set's got to change *first*, or nothing will change."

I can second these thoughts on mind-set. I will see a podcaster who is thrilled with their downloads and overjoyed with their progress—until they see someone else's numbers. Then the air is let out of the balloon, the confidence evaporates, and thoughts turn to quitting. DO NOT COMPARE YOURSELF TO OTHERS.

Instead, stay locked on your audience and what they need. They put blinders on horses competing in a race. This blocks them from seeing what is behind them, and what is beside them, and keeps them locked on the finish line. The finish line is developing a relationship with your audience that leads them to want to give you money.

Conclusion

I want to thank you for buying this book. I hope you found it of value. I hope it sparked some ideas in your brain. Above all, I hope you see that successful podcasts are built by delivering value and creating relationships. Step one is to grow your audience. Without an audience, there is no monetization.

Writing this book was not easy. It took a lot of effort. It took a lot of focus. It took a lot of discipline, and now I have the experience of writing a book with a publisher, and nobody can take that away.

With talent, dedication, discipline, and some luck, you can end up being an influencer. Keep your eye on the long game and do those things that large podcasters can't do when you're small. Engage your audience (don't wait for them to engage you). It takes courage because you might reach out to the audience and find no one is there. Do it anyway. If you've done the homework of identifying your target audience and understanding what they want, there is going to be someone there.

Realize that some ideas and insights only come by jumping into your niche and finding out what they need. I do know this; you're not going to help anyone with your recordings sitting on your hard drive. I know so many people who are seeing results after sitting on their microphone for years. Don't be one of those people who looks back and says, "Oh, if I had only started this sooner . . ."

Get out there and start changing your world, one download at a time. If you get stuck, you know where to find me.

APPENDIX
Tools

I'm going to include some tools that I use, or are used by people I know. This is a book, and the minute I publish it, there may be more or better resources. For the most up-to-date version of this list, see profitfromyourpodcast.com/resources.

SPEAKING RESOURCES

These are the type of sites where you sign up and make a profile. You will get emails (or search their site) for events that might fit your content.

SpeakerHub

I've used this site to find a few speaking gigs. According to their website, "We believe in the power of live presentations and personal connections, which is why we created SpeakerHub. We are not a speaker agency but the fastest-growing community of professional, independent, or amateur public speakers and trainers who'd like to be found by companies, event organizers, and schools. We welcome anyone with expertise in any field who is open to speaking at conferences, events or schools as a paid or pro bono presenter."

See podclick.me/speakerhub.

My Speaking Agent

This is a simple, free site. When I logged in, I was surprised to find a free service that posted a lot of events of which I had not heard. According to their website, "Agent gives you access to 1,000+ conferences and the contact info of the decision makers."

See podclick.me/myspeakingagent.

SELLING YOUR OWN PRODUCTS

When it comes to selling your own products, many of these will be digital. There are so many tools to choose. One word of advice is to go for the tools that have the features you need. You may be dazzled by all the options of a product (that you don't need). You end up buying a product that does more, but those extra options now make more of a learning curve.

Gumroad

I created a spreadsheet that enables you to track your own *Biggest Loser*-style weight-loss competition (I created this in about fifteen minutes). I marketed it on my *Logical Weight Loss* podcast. I charge $10. People are willing pay $10 to avoid having to do all the math. Last year, I made $740 selling a spreadsheet people could make for free. To sell this spreadsheet, I used Gumroad. It's simple and affordable. You can accept payments from all major credit cards, including Visa, MasterCard, American Express, Discover, Diners Club, and JCB, as well as PayPal.

You can create subscriptions, coupons, and even rentals (for those offering videos). If you are worried about people stealing or sharing your ebook, they have built-in abuse prevention, but you can turn off downloads for your product, or let them stamp a PDF you're selling for each customer.

In addition to digital goods, you can sell physical goods as well. This includes features for shipping as well as tax collection.

You can start for free; the professional features start at ten dollars a month. Their price includes unlimited bandwidth, and payments are just 3.5% + 30¢ per charge.

If you're looking for a simple, safe, solution to sell a product (that doesn't cost and arm and a leg), this is a good place to start.

See podclick.me/gumroad.

Sam Cart

Sam Cart is a shopping cart for information marketers and Internet marketers selling digital products online. Sam Cart has all sorts of bells and whistles. Customers can add additional products on the fly. You can add upsells (so after someone buys a product you can offer a "one-time" offer). There is also an A/B testing feature that lets you test different versions of your product listing so you can choose the one that is converting the best.

It is geared toward marketers, so it integrates with email programs as well as Zapier (which enables it to integrate with a ton of other platforms). It also has plenty of tools for revenue, including coupons, membership/subscriptions, trial offers, coupons, and payment plans. It can even create checkout pop-ups to make it easy to have a pop-up box right on your website.

It has a built-in affiliate tool to create your own affiliate program and has good reporting. Sam Cart takes zero fees (except for that $99 monthly fee).

See podclick.me/samcart.

Shopify Cart System

Shopify is another great tool. I've not used this one myself, but I know a few people who adore it. It is almost its own ecosystem at this point. In the same way that the free software Audacity has its own community, Shopify is becoming so universal that it's not hard to find a guru (and I hear their own support is great). I mean, they even have their own podcast at www.shopify.com/podcasts as well as an academy to help you get the most of out the platform at www.shopify.com/academy.

Pricing starts at $9 a month with Shopify Lite. It allows you to sell on Facebook and chat with your customers on Messenger, add products to any website or blog, and accept credit card payments. The next "regular" plan is $29/month.

See podclick.me/shopify.

Thrive Cart

It is almost easier to say what Thrive Cart does NOT do than to say what it does. I use this for my *Podcast Review Show*. If people order a review, they sign up and are taken to a form created by Thrive Cart where they fill in data that I need to conduct my review. It works with PayPal and Stripe for payment processing. At the time of this writing, if you are running a membership site, Thrive Cart will natively integrate with WishList Member, Digital Access Pass, MemberMouse, OptimizeMember, and Teachable.

It handles your taxes; it has a built-in affiliate program. If you have multiple sites you can set up the cart with products on one site, and then have additional products for a second website, and use the cart on both. There are also no restrictions on the number of products you can create.

If you are selling software that requires upgrade management, it can do that. It does retargeting (for those using Facebook), video carts, and as I said, I think it's easier to list what it does not do (currently it will not do your laundry, but it is in development). My biggest complaint is it goes on and off the market. Their support is there, but for some reason, you need to sign up and be notified when it goes live. As I've tried other carts, this was ridiculously easy for such a powerful system.

See podclick.me/thrivecart.

Easy Digital Downloads

If you are using WordPress, it's easy on the wallet to start selling with this free plug-in. From ebooks, to WordPress plug-ins, to PDF files and more, Easy Digital Downloads makes selling digital products a breeze. Easy Digital Downloads is simple to use and free to download. If you're saying, "What's the catch?" it is that its free version only works with PayPal standard. If you are using PayPal Pro or want to use something such as Stripe, you must pay, but the nice thing about this configuration is you're only paying for the features you need. It has a full system to manage customers, reporting, and more. You can see what features you need at easydigitaldownloads.com/downloads/. For example, the PayPal Pro addition is $89/year. To encourage you to buy in bundles they do have different packages at a more affordable rate that include multiple gateways as well as additional features for $199/year.

See podclick.me/easydigitaldownloads.

MEMBERSHIP SITE TOOLS

I provided some tips on how to run a membership site, here are some of the top tools to help you administer your own. You can have a website, a feed, or even make your own version of Netflix.

Membership Academy

The Membership Academy is one of the most focused websites around memberships I've ever seen. I signed up for one item. They had a resource that compared all the different membership tools on one spreadsheet. I signed up and stayed for years. Mike and Callie are 100 percent transparent and share all the information they learn from working with so many people who have membership sites. You will learn to measure your churn rate and run your membership site like a business so you can identify problems and adjust to keep your members happy.

They are NOT sleazy Internet marketers helping you get rich quick (can you tell why I like them?). The academy is a huge value for the price you pay, and they have an active forum that allows you to network with other membership site owners.

Check them out at podclick.me/membershipacademy.

Digital Access Pass

This tool works on WordPress sites (or non-WordPress sites). It is one of the most versatile membership sites and can lock down your content so nobody can get to it. If you don't want to use Patreon, Digital Access Pass (DAP) can do the same thing (and cut out the middleman). It can create secure RSS feeds, and if someone quits paying, they lose access to your content. If you go to their features page, you'd better get comfortable. It really does everything and integrates with everything. They offer a one-time fee for those who want to buy the script/plug-in, but they offer some great features and coaching for those that do a monthly subscription that is much more affordable than many "course creation" tools. I've known the people behind the tool, and their support is amazing (and they are always listening and always adding more features).

Check it out at podclick.me/dap.

Thinkific vs. Teachable

Thinkific and Teachable are two of the top tools for creating online courses. They are very close in their feature set. If you are comparing them, look at the packages for $99/month. Yes, that's a bit much when you are first starting, but if things go well you're going to end up with this plan. This strategy will enable you to compare each platform on a more even level.

Here are some things I've spotted.

Thinkific

Thinkific's course-building is robust with the ability to copy lessons between courses, and they have course templates and provide hints to help you make courses to better facilitate education.

If you're new to making videos, Thinkific has a tool to allow you to do "voice-over PowerPoint" and make great-looking videos.

Thinkific also allows you to set the first lesson of a course to be viewed for free.

Thinkific's free plan lets you get started and doesn't limit the number of students (Teachable limits your student body to ten people when you are on the free plan).

If you are looking for more control over your site design, Thinkific is more powerful. This doesn't mean Teachable sites look bad, but Thinkific gives you more tools.

I use Thinkific for the School of Podcasting. The thing that attracted me was I heard the founder on a podcast (of course), and he explained how this was built for education. So many scripts and a ton of features are created and used by developers who think they are great. Thinkific is created with the goal of education. Yes, it has marketing tools and integrations, but at its core, it's about education. I love that it integrates with ConvertKit, but it also integrates with Zapier, which somewhat means it works with everything.

I love the Thinkific video library, which makes it easy to use videos in multiple lessons.

Thinkific doesn't charge any transaction fees.

Thinkific's quizzes allow you to add images and videos, which can help students understand the questions (Teachable currently just has plain text for quiz questions).

Thinkific offers an Assignments feature in their courses that allows you to accept submissions from your students. Plus, you can also accept/reject their submissions.

If you are just crushing it, Thinkific has a "groups" feature that allows you to sell courses to organizations. It is part of their growth package (so you will need to upgrade).

Their support is great, and their feature set is solid.

Teachable

I have experienced Teachable more as a student than an admin (although I have played with their free version). Their interface is very simple and easy to use.

Teachable offers an app where your students can log in and take the course (and Thinkific does not). This is a pretty cool feature. While Thinkific courses are mobile friendly, that is still slightly different than a full-fledged app.

Every review I've read online has stated that while Thinkific has a more robust system when it comes to creating courses, Teachable is still powerful and easier to use. Teachable, for example, allows you to import content from Dropbox or Google Drive.

If you're looking for your audience to WATCH the videos, Teachable will lock the content until the student has watched the video.

The Bottom Line with Thinkific vs. Teachable

For course creation, either one is a good choice. Teachable offers a more flexible course builder and an iOS app for your students and a better system for leaving comments and instigating discussions. This will depend if you want your lessons to be "robust." Most people just have videos and such (so it's a bit of a tie).

If you're going to be doing a lot of quizzing, Thinkific has a more robust quizzing feature, an assignments feature, better surveys, and the "Groups" feature. For me, I give this to Thinkific.

Regarding design, Teachable looks modern but lacks some of the flexibility of Thinkific. Thinkific's drag-and-drop page builder has more flexibility than Teachable. For design, the winner is Thinkific.

When it comes to marketing, Teachable has an edge with a slick one-step checkout phase. Thinkific has a two-step phase. Both allow you to have one-click upsells. Teachable has a customizable thank-you page that can include video. This one is all Teachable.

Regarding getting paid, you get instant payouts on all plans in Thinkific. While on Teachable, you get instant payouts on all plans only if you're in the United States or Canada. Otherwise, you'll get instant payouts only on $99/month and above plans. Teachable also has its own payment gateway. Using this you can accept credit card (or PayPal) payments even if Stripe (or PayPal) isn't supported in your country. Something like this wouldn't be possible if you were using Thinkific. You can also accept payments via Apple Pay and Google Pay. I mentioned the BackOffice feature that will help you pay affiliates and handle taxes for the EU VAT. If you use Teachable's gateway instead of your own Stripe/PayPal accounts, they will even pay the tax to the respective authorities on your behalf. This seems like a win for Teachable.

Both have affiliate programs, but Teachable can adjust the cookie length. Teachable's affiliate program works even if your landing pages aren't on Teachable. As someone who uses Thinkific's affiliate program, I can say almost anything will beat it. It works, but it's a very minimal product. This one goes to Teachable.

For integrations, both can be tied into Zapier (which allows you to integrate it with a ton of services). Thinkific integrates with more email tools (Teachable only integrates with ConvertKit and MailChimp).

As you can see, it is hard to decide between these two. Thinkific has a more robust course builder. If your courses don't need to be that robust, that may not be an issue. Teachable has a better checkout and more sales and marketing tools.

All this to say, the best thing is to go sign up for a free account and play around.

- Thinkific: podclick.me/thinkific
- Teachable: podclick.me/teachable

PRIVATE RSS FEEDS

If you like the idea of a Patreon-type experience for your audience, but you're not a fan of patreon.com, here are some alternatives:

MyLibsyn

If you want to setup a Netflix-type system, the MyLibsyn option is a nice "Set it and forget it" system. With no up-front costs and just a simple revenue share, podcast producers can quickly monetize audio and video content, PDFs, back catalogs, and bonus episodes. Your subscribers sign up and create one username and password and can access their subscription across all available (custom) apps and your branded premium page. No matter your audience's device preference, access to your premium content is easy and secure. Subscribers can easily unlock content they have paid for via mobile apps for Android and iOS. Individual developer fees apply.

Depending on the number of active subscribers, Libsyn takes between 20 and 30 percent. While that may seem higher than others, any customer issues can go right to Libsyn support (all the forgotten passwords, credit card issues etc., are all handled by Libsyn). In full disclosure, I am part of the Libsyn support team. Also, if you choose to have a custom app created, Libsyn will update the app to work with future versions of the different operating systems.

See podclick.me/mylibsyn.

The Supporting Cast

This is a pretty slick tool, as instead of people having to use another app or having to learn how to manually subscribe to a feed in their favorite app, Supporting Cast makes it easy. Upon receiving payment, it takes the customer to a page where they can subscribe to your private member-only feed *in their favorite app*. There is one fee (not tiers like Patreon), and you get ad-free episodes and bonus content. This is for the person who has an audience that wants more content.

They take 15 percent, and you get paid via Stripe.

See podclick.me/supportingcastfm.

Supercast

Supercast focuses on making a private podcast simple. They host your files (and provide stats) and make it super easy for your audience. When they click a link on your site, they choose their plan, and then ask what app on their phone they use to listen to podcasts (and they use the personalized rss feed to manually subscribe if their app isn't listed. They charge $.059 per member per month plus 2.9% + $0.30 per transaction. They also accept payment in CAD, USD, EUR, and GBP. Their system makes a landing page for you and has a built-in "Ask me anything" system for your members to ask you questions.

Found out more at podclick.me/supercast.

Memberful

Memberful is owned by Patreon. If you wanted a membership site without the Patreon branding, Memberful provides that. They charge 10% on the starter plan, or $25/month plus a 4.9% transaction fee on their pro plan. Their pro plan provides coupon codes, custom branding and more. Memberful does NOT host your media. You enter your feed, and they create a personalized version for each member. Keep in mind that you will need a media host and want to budget in their fee as part of the equation (where supercast is a media host for private podcasts and provides unique feeds). Memberful does provide a way to upload episodes manually so you can embed a player on your website (and in that way they do provide hosting - for players - not for feeds).

For more information see podclick.me/memberful.

Please let me know if you have any additional questions.

BuyMeACoffee.com

This site is dedicated to going to "extreme lengths to make it easy for creators to get started, and for their audience to support them." Their interface is super easy to use, and they provide easy tools to integrate this into your website. They charge 5 percent, plus PayPal and Stripe processing fees. All payments are instantly transferred to the connected accounts. Their website states, "Unlike other platforms, we do not hold your balance, and there is no minimum threshold." They are adding ways to sell swag and create members-only content.

See podclick.me/buymeacoffee.

MERCHANDISE/SWAG

If you're looking to promote your business on a shirt, mug, sticker, or back window, here are some tools to investigate.

TeePublic

I've been using TeePublic for a few years. I really like their shirts, and the designs feel great and don't fall apart after two trips through the washing machine. The nice thing about TeePublic is you can put other artist's shirts in your store, and you earn a commission. You could have an audience member create a design and put it in your store. Then you can feature it in your store (and you both get paid).

They also do many different items including wall hangings, mugs, wall art, phone cases, stickers, and many different styles of shirts and hoodies.

See podclick.me/teepublic.

Sticker Mule

I've used stickermule.com for stickers, coasters, and some vinyl letters to put in the back window of my car with my domain on it. Their quality is good. Their interface is super easy, and if you are on their email list, they send out special deals from time to time. If you're looking for stickers, magnets, buttons, mailers, coasters, wall graphics, window stickers, and more, they have a wide selection and good pricing.

See podclick.me/stickermule.

AFFILIATE TOOLS

I previously mentioned Skimlinks.com in the chapter about affiliate marketing; here are some more affiliate tools.

Kit.co

Kit.co is a website that is great for those who want to sell bundles of products. They work with affiliate programs from Amazon, B&H Photo, eBay, Newegg, and FlipKart. You put in your identify information (so for Amazon, your tracking ID) and you can create bundles of products. This is great for me as I have kits for the solo podcaster as well as kits for "podcasting on the road." People can look at the products (with descriptions you create, as you know the way to inspire your audience), and if they want them all, Kit.co provides a button to buy them all (I do believe the different products have to be from the same vendor).

How do you get paid? If someone purchases through your affiliate link you will get paid the same way you always do. If you are an Amazon affiliate, the affiliate sale is tracked by Amazon, and you are paid via Amazon.

So how does kit.co make money? According to their website, "We're focused on making the best home for the products worth getting. We're creatives ourselves, so we fundamentally believe in creator-friendly policies—which is why we want you to keep 100 percent of the revenue you generate." (Yeah, it's unheard of.) In the instance where a creator does not have his or her own affiliate ID or does not wish to use one, Kit will use its own.

Geniuslink

As podcasting has a global audience, Geniuslink stops the days of you leaving "money on the table." According to their website, "With Geniuslink you don't waste hours manually editing links or hunting down your affiliate IDs. Just copy, paste, and your links are optimized and ready to go. Once you add your affiliate IDs the first time, Geniuslink instantly affiliates any link to Amazon, iTunes, Walmart, and more. Geniuslink detects a shopper's country, language, device, and more, then routes them to the best page for them. It's automatic for Amazon, iTunes, and Microsoft. Plus, you can define custom destinations for any other affiliate program."

If you're like me, you are thinking, *Okay, how much does this cost?* Plans start at $9/month. The more clicks you need, the more it costs.

See podclick.me/geniuslink.

EasyAzon

EasyAzon is a piece of cake for Amazon affiliates. You drop in your affiliate ID, and the rest is super easy. According to their website, "EasyAzon 4 has a built-in automatic link localizer that will take your Amazon affiliate link and display a link for the Amazon locale based on who is visiting your website. Check one single box in the EasyAzon 4 settings to automatically localize your affiliate links and cash in on wasted international traffic. If a user clicks through your affiliate link and adds an item to their shopping cart you have an extra eight-nine days to get a commission if they buy the item they added. This is a single purchase (instead of a monthly payment)."

See podclick.me/easyazon.

MISCELLANEOUS TOOL FOR YOUR BUSINESS

Here are some tools I've used myself to help my run and promote my business.

Freshbooks

I use Freshbooks for my invoicing. I love that it sends reminders and (if I want) charges late fees for those clients that don't pay. I track all my expenses, and I can easily see how my business is doing. It also has a timer feature if you bill by the minute.

See podclick.me/freshbooks.

Freshdesk

Having Freshdesk and Freshbooks gets a bit confusing. Freshdesk is a ticketing and knowledge-base system that is free. If you have products, you need to support them, and this is a great tool to help you do that. The knowledge-base helps you cut down on tickets, and the ticketing system makes sure all questions get handled. While they have a paid version, all the features I need are covered under the Freshdesk free plan.

See podclick.me/freshdesk.

Acuity Scheduling

I use this to schedule my consulting calls. It seamlessly works with Freshbooks and my Google Calendar so that someone can go to my calendar, pick a time, pay for the appointment, and it creates a paid invoice in my Freshbooks. It integrates with zoom.us (a video conferencing tool), so it also creates the meeting. If you want to set up subscriptions, or set up tickets for an event, it can all be done with Acuity. Lastly, their customer support is like none I've ever seen.

Gone are the days where there was confusion due to time zones. Gone are the days where people didn't pay their invoices.

See podclick.me/acuityscheduling.

Manage WP

If you have multiple websites running WordPress, this is an amazing tool. When I log in, it checks all my sites. It then lets me know if there are any plug-ins or themes that need updating. I just logged into my account and I have twenty-four plug-ins, four themes, and one WordPress install that need updating across my twelve websites. I have 6,000 spam messages on those sites. I can accomplish all my updates with two mouse clicks. It also will back up my website. A large portion of this is free, and the paid tools are inexpensive.

See: podclick.me/managewp.

About the Author

Dave Jackson is an award-winning 2018 Podcasters Hall of Fame inductee who has been helping people to understand technology and harness its power for over twenty years. He is best known for launching the School of Podcasting in 2005. In his fifteen years of podcasting, he has launched over thirty podcasts himself with over four million downloads. He is also a featured speaker at podcast events, a contributor to the *Podcast Business Journal*, and a member of the libsyn.com support team. His experience, position, and channels allow him to help more podcasters than anyone else on the planet. He lives in Akron, Ohio. When Dave isn't podcasting . . . wait . . . Dave is always podcasting. Find him at www.schoolofpodcasting.com and find all of his podcasting shows at www.powerofpodcasting.com.

Index

Books from Allworth Press

Blog for Bucks
by Jacqueline Bodnar (6 × 9, 168 pages, paperback, $16.99)

Brand Thinking and Other Noble Pursuits
by Debbie Millman with foreword by Rob Walker (6 × 9, 336 pages, paperback, $19.95)

Branding for Bloggers
by Zach Heller with the New York Institute of Career Development (5½ × 8¼, 112 pages, paperback, $16.95)

Feng Shui and Money (Second Edition)
by Eric Shaffert (6 × 9, 256 pages, paperback, $19.99)

From Idea to Exit (Revised Edition)
by Jeffrey Weber (6 × 9, 272 pages, paperback, $19.95)

Fund Your Dreams Like a Creative Genius™
by Brainard Carey (6⅛ × 6⅛, 160 pages, paperback, $12.99)

The Global PR Revolution
by Maxim Behar (6 × 9, 312 pages, hardcover, $29.99)

The Law (in Plain English)® for Small Business (Fifth Edition)
by Leonard D. DuBoff and Amanda Bryan (6 × 9, 312 pages, paperback, $24.99)

Legal Guide to Social Media
by Kimberly A. Houser (6 × 9, 208 pages, paperback, $19.95)

Millennial Rules
by T. Scott Gross (6 × 9, 176 pages, paperback, $16.95)

The Money Mentor
by Tad Crawford (6 × 9, 272 pages, paperback, $24.95)

The Online Writer's Companion
by P. J. Aitken (6 × 9, 344 pages, paperback, $19.99)

The Profitable Artist (Second Edition)
by The New York Foundation for the Arts (6 × 9, 288 pages, paperback, $24.99)

The Secret Life of Money
by Tad Crawford (5½ × 8½, 304 pages, paperback, $19.95)

Sell Online Like a Creative Genius™
by Brainard Carey (6⅛× 6⅛, 160 pages, paperback, $12.99)

Starting Your Career as a Freelance Writer (Third Edition)
by Moira Allen (6 × 9, 368 pages, paperback, $19.99)

Succeed with Social Media Like a Creative Genius™
by Brainard Carey (6⅛ × 6⅛, 144 pages, paperback, $12.99)

There's Money Where Your Mouth Is (Fourth Edition)
by Elaine A. Clark (6 × 9, 360 pages, paperback, $24.99)

VO
by Harlan Hogan (6 × 9, 256 pages, paperback, $19.95)

Website Branding for Small Businesses
by Nathalie Nahai (6 × 9, 288 pages, paperback, $19.95)

To see our complete catalog or to order online, please visit www.allworth.com.